EMBROIDERY

 VAN NOSTRAND REINHOLD COMPANY

NEW YORK   CINCINNATI   TORONTO   LONDON   MELBOURNE

in association with Phoebus

Editor: Mary Harding
Assistant Editor: Margo Coughtrie
Editorial Assistants: Sally Fisher, Kitsa Caswell
Consultants: Patsy North, Greta Barrett
Design Coordinator: Jan Churcher
Production Control: Sheila Biddlecombe
Editorial Director: Graham Donaldson

INTRODUCTION

Embroidery has existed as a decorative art for as long as man has been able to create yarns and fabrics, and many richly-worked heirlooms still exist to remind us of the skill of our ancestors. In today's machine age, embroidery is particularly highly-prized as no factory-made article can replace the charm of a hand-worked piece. Embroidery is high-fashion, too, with the revival of the peasant look in flowered smocks and blouses or the elegance of a personal monogram on a silk shirt or scarf.

This book contains a wealth of beautiful designs for the embroidery enthusiast. It is divided into two sections — one for the home and one for the family. In the first, there are crisp linen tablecloths, colorful cushions, delicate net curtains; in the second, stunning blouses, designs for knitwear, and a number of small designs and alphabets that will enliven plain clothes.

The range of techniques covers simple cross, satin, and chain stitch right through to intricate drawn-thread work, so beginners and experts alike will find plenty to suit their capabilities. New techniques are clearly-explained with step-by-step photographs and actual-size trace patterns or simple charts of the designs are given, so you will achieve results to be proud of every time. The patterns in this book will prove to be a constant source of inspiration and, who knows, you may find you are creating the heirlooms of the future.

CONTENTS

The traditional blue onion design has been reproduced for you as an embroidery pattern for a white tablecloth. Set a festive table with a pretty blue-and-white tea set.

Inspired by
a design on china

Embroidery in blue

Materials Required: Stranded cotton: 11 skeins dark blue, 5 skeins pale blue. Linen tablecloth.

Embroidering the motifs

Mark the center of the cloth with horizontal and vertical lines of basting stitches in pastel-colored thread. Trace the motifs and transfer them onto the linen with dressmaker's carbon paper. The large floral motif is positioned in the center and the small onion motifs form a border. On the cloth illustrated, the distance from the center to the border is 44 cm (17½″) on the long sides and 25 cm (10″) on the short sides. The onion motifs are about 2 cm (¾″) apart. Arrange the small flower motifs inside the border. Work the outlines in stem stitch and fill in the leaves and flowers with satin stitch worked in the colors shown in the illustrations.

The graceful flower motif is worked with subtle shading in only two blues.

Motifs used to be transferred onto fabric by painting through a copper stencil with a stiff brush.

Motif revival

These delicate copper stencils were used in the past to transfer embroidery designs onto fabric. The dressmaker's carbon paper method is more common nowadays, so we have reproduced several of the traditional designs for you to use as trace patterns. Here they are embroidered onto tea towels, but you can also use them on other household linen or clothes and accessories.

A selection of the traditional motifs which were cut into copper stencils.

Materials Required: Selection of tea towels. Stranded embroidery cotton in red. Dressmaker's carbon paper. Embroidery frame.

Basic Stitches: Stem stitch for fine lines, satin stitch for small leaves. Dots, larger leaves, wider lines, and the alphabet are padded with one or more rows of chain stitch first, then they are covered with satin stitch. Use buttonhole stitch for the scalloped borders.

Working the embroidery

The various motifs are given actual size on the pattern. Decide where you want to position each motif and transfer to the fabric with dressmaker's carbon paper. Make sure that continuous borders follow on in a straight line. Transfer the scalloped edgings slightly in from the edge of the fabric; the surplus fabric is cut off later. For letters I and Y, use J and Z without the crosslines.

Work the embroidery in the Basic Stitches, using 4 strands. Press on wrong side under a damp cloth when finished.

A. G.
B. H.
C. J.
D. K.
E. L.
F. M.

N. T.
O. U.
P. V.
Q. W.
R. H.
S. Z.

Trace these patterns to transfer the delicate designs onto fabric. For letters I and Y, use letters J and Z without the fine crosslines.

In keeping with tradition

A traditional pattern in blue on white always makes an inviting table setting. We've matched the motif on the cloth to the design on the china — a clever idea for you to try sometime with your own tableware or any favorite china pattern.

The tablecloth illustrated is square with the main motif in the centre and a border all around the edge.

Size of cloth: 150 cm (59") square.

Materials Required:
White linen: 160 cm (63") square. Stranded cotton: 17 skeins blue.

Making the cloth
Turn a 5 cm (2") hem to the right side, mitering the corners. Turn in the raw edge and stitch the hem close to the edge.

Mark the center of the cloth horizontally and vertically with basting. Trace the central motif ($\frac{1}{2}$ is given on the pattern) and transfer to the cloth with dressmaker's carbon paper. Distribute the 8 small motifs evenly around the central motif as shown in the small photograph on the far right. Place the border motifs so that the outer edge of the motifs is 16 cm ($6\frac{1}{4}$") from the edge of the cloth, making sure that they are equidistant. Place a corner motif at each corner as shown right.

Working the embroidery

With undivided strands, the lines are worked in stem stitch, the large dots in satin stitch, the small dots with French knots.

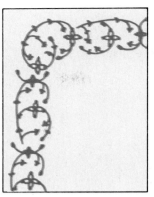
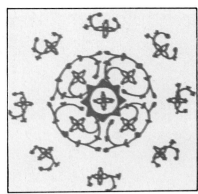

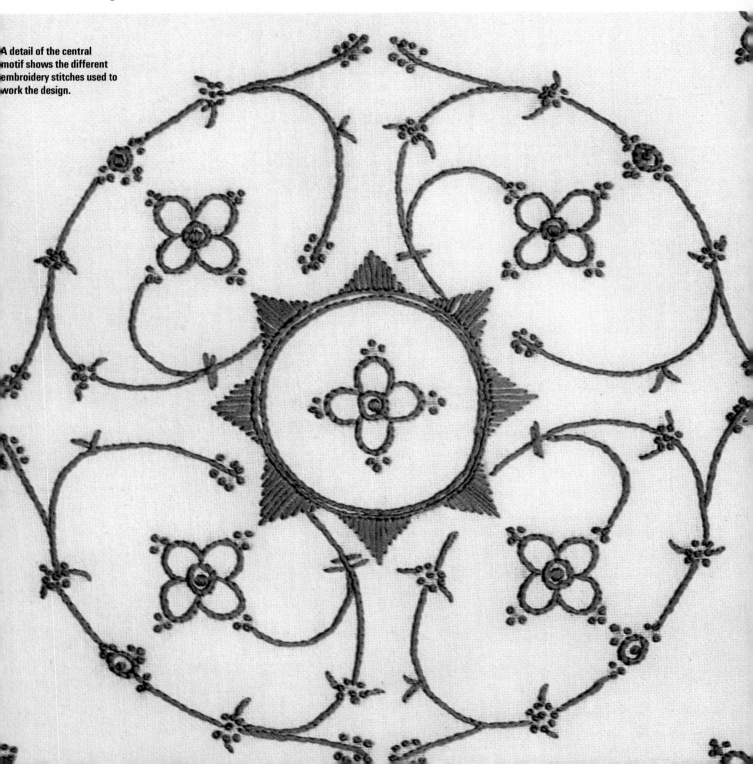

A detail of the central motif shows the different embroidery stitches used to work the design.

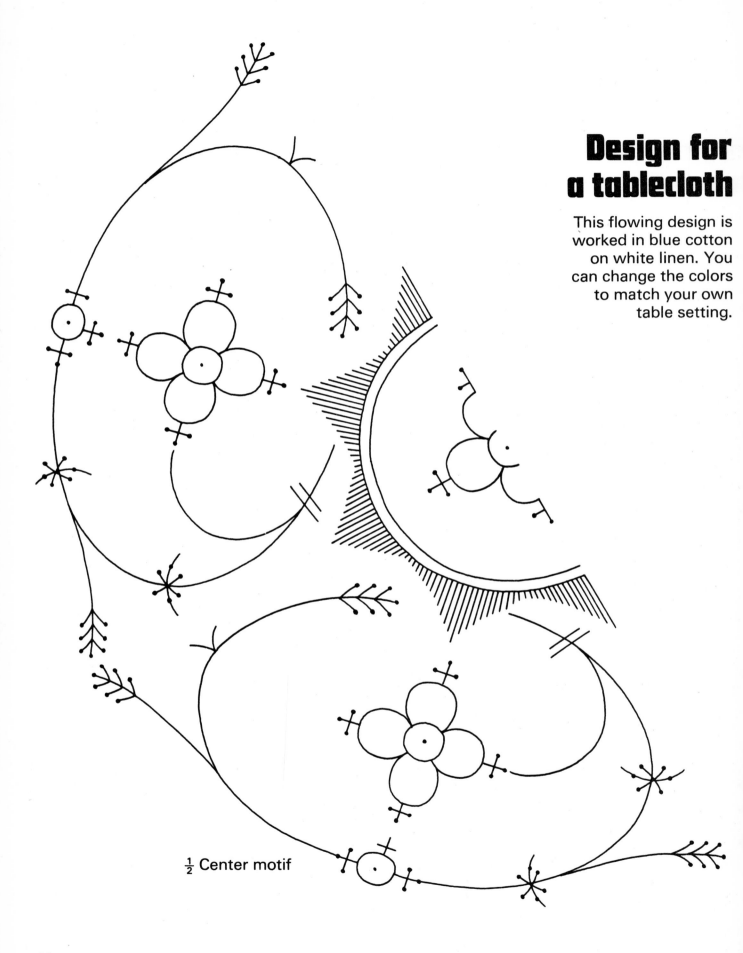

Design for a tablecloth

This flowing design is worked in blue cotton on white linen. You can change the colors to match your own table setting.

½ Center motif

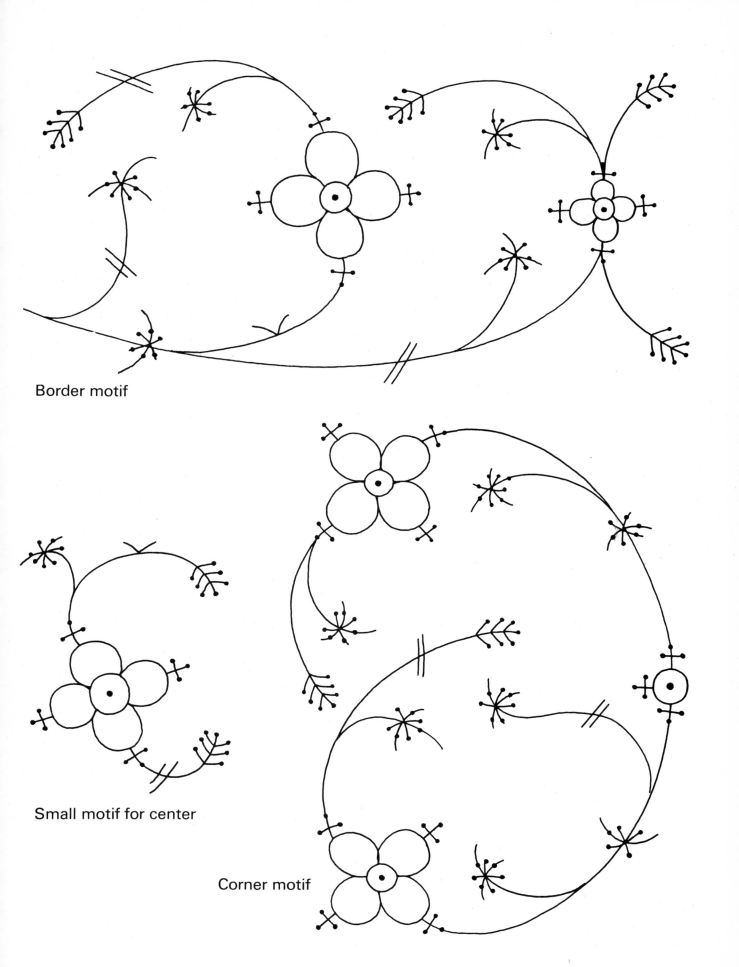

Border motif

Small motif for center

Corner motif

Ice crystals and stars

Decorate a linen table runner with ice crystals in three shades of blue. Group motifs as shown and work two rows of chain stitch for the border.

A single motif and chain stitch border will enhance a breakfast set.

Marking design on fabric

The ice crystal motif at left is actual size. Trace the motif onto transparent paper and transfer it to fabric with dressmaker's tracing paper in a contrasting color. Place the dressmaker's tracing paper face down on the right side of the fabric. Place traced motif on top and, holding both firmly in position, go over the lines of the design with a pencil or a dry ball-point pen. Use a single motif or arrange motifs in a group. Trace the motif as many times as required. The lines will be covered with embroidery and will not show.

Embroidering the motif

Use pearl cotton or three strands of stranded embroidery cotton. Work the straight lines of the design in chain stitch and the petal shapes in lazy daisy stitch.

A milky way of stars in glowing golds and bronzes or a crisp pattern of ice crystals in frosty blues to embroider in simple chain stitch.

Marking design on fabric

Trace stars and mark them on fabric as for ice crystal embroidery. The tablecloth illustrated here has a wide band of stars embroidered across the center. The motifs could also be grouped in a wide border for a circular cloth or as a large central motif. A pretty effect could also be achieved by sprinkling the stars at random all over the cloth.

Embroidering the stars

Use pearl cotton or three strands of stranded embroidery cotton. Choose four or five colors in the yellow to bronze range. Work each star outline with two rows of chain stitch. The first is worked on the design line and the second outside it.

Pressing embroidery

Place embroidered piece face down on a well-padded surface and press with a steam iron or a dry iron and a damp cloth. Work from the center outward and press lightly so the stitching will not be flattened. Remember that pressing is not ironing. Raise and lower the iron with a gentle motion. Press in direction of the grain.

Fruit and vegetables to appliqué

Apply yourself

These appliqué motifs are a real feast for the eyes! Cut from scraps of cotton, they are outlined in blanket stitch with details in satin and stem stitch and French knots.

Size: The place mat illustrated measures 50 cm x 35 cm (19⅝" x 13¾").

Materials Required: (for 2 place mats) Linen: 1.20 m (1⅜ yds), 90 cm (36") wide. Piping: 3 m (3¼ yds). Cotton remnants. Oddments of stranded cotton. Fine iron-on interfacing.

Making the mats
All the fruit on these two pages is shown actual size. Trace the separate pieces onto tracing paper and transfer them onto the adhesive side of the interfacing with dressmaker's carbon paper. Cut them out and iron them onto the relevant fabric remnants. Where two shapes overlap, add 0.5 cm (¼") seam allowance on the underlap. Where two shapes of the same fabric meet, cut out the two parts together rather than separately and embroider the separating lines in stem stitch in the same color as on the pineapple leaves or carrots. Use 3 strands of cotton for the embroidery. The appliqué edging is worked in blanket stitch. All lines on the motifs are in stem stitch; smaller areas such as stems, shoots, or grass in satin stitch. The dots on the orange and the onion are French knots. To finish the mats, turn hem to right side, mitering the corners. Turn in seam allowance and stitch, catching in the piping.

For clothes, tablecloths, and bed linen **Add a colored border**

If you are a romantic at heart, then these embroidered borders will appeal to you. Choose your favorite motif — the simple flowers, the intricate arabesques, or the stylized bouquets — then add a scalloped border.

The petals and leaves of these small flowers are worked in satin stitch. They look charming around the yoke of a dress or blouse and can be repeated at the edge of the sleeves.

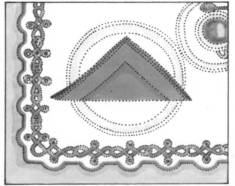

A border of arabesques has a timeless beauty. It looks decorative on place mats, but could equally well be worked all around the edge of a tablecloth. The border is worked in satin stitch.

Plain white pillows are given an individual touch with a border of stylized bouquets worked in lazy daisy or detached chain stitch. They would make a guest room look charming and inviting.

These sprays of roses are worked in satin stitch, the rows of dots around the edge in French knots. They make a delightful border on the turn-over of a sheet for a child's bed. The scalloped edge on the borders is worked in buttonhole stitch.

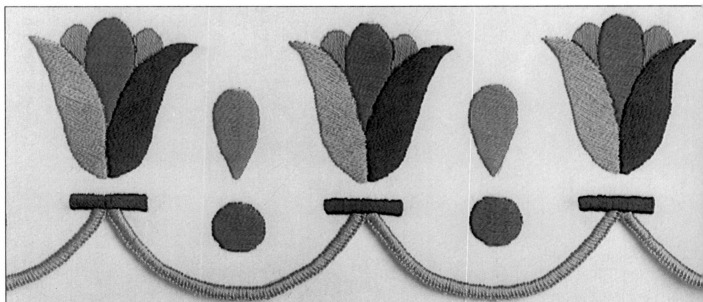

The stylized tulips are worked in satin stitch, using several different colors of stranded cotton. The decorative scallops are worked in buttonhole stitch

Materials Required:

Stranded embroidery cotton in the following colors and quantities for 40 cm (15¾") of border. Purple border: 1 skein purple, ½ skein green. Red border: 2 skeins red. Blue border: ½ skein each of pale blue and dark blue. Pink border: 1 skein salmon pink, ½ skein green. Tulip border: 1 skein each of pale blue, dark blue, pale green, and dark green. Fabric: Any closely-woven cotton or linen.

Tracing the borders

The pattern shows a section of each border including a corner. Before you transfer the border onto the fabric, work out the required length and adjust so that the repeated motifs meet exactly at the corners. Transfer with dressmaker's carbon paper.

Working the embroidery

Purple border: Work the petals and leaves in satin stitch with 2 strands, the stems in stem stitch with 3 strands and the dots in French knots.

Red border: Work in satin stitch with 2 strands.

Blue border: The petals and leaves are lazy daisies, the dots are French knots, all using 2 strands. The inner scallops are worked in satin stitch with 3 strands.

Rose border: Work the petals and leaves in satin stitch with 2 strands, the French knots with 3 strands.

Tulip border: All the motifs are worked in satin stitch with 2 strands. Use diagonal stitches for the outer petals, horizontal stitches for the center petal and the small motifs, and vertical stitches for the small petals and the lines above the scallops.

Scalloped edges: The outer edges are worked with 3 strands in buttonhole stitch over a running stitch outline filled with padding stitches. Cut away fabric carefully close to stitches.

Embroidery on borders

Looped motifs in satin stitch

1 Work around the double lines of the motifs, but where one line crosses under another, leave a space and continue on the other side. The space will be filled in later.

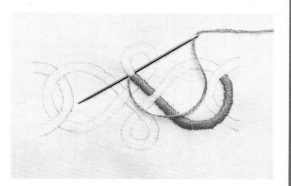

2 As you continue around, you will meet lines that are already embroidered. Do not embroider over them, but continue working on the other side of them. Where the lines cross, the stitches will lie in opposite directions, to give the impression of a looped ribbon.

Lines of French knots

1 Bring the thread through the fabric and wind it three times around the needle tip from front to back. The working thread must be held taut while making the knot.

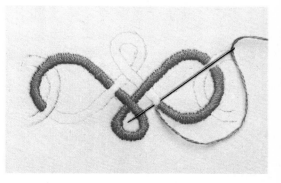

2 Still holding the thread, insert again close to where it first emerged. Bring the needle out at the next dot and continue as before.

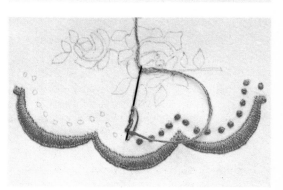

Scalloped borders

Give a colorful finish to clothes and linens with any one of these decorative edgings.

Here you can see exactly how the lines of braid cross one another.

A detail of the corner motif of the design.

Arabesque borders

Beautifully braided

Decorative braid work is a lovely old technique often found in traditional peasant embroidery.

Size: The cloth illustrated measures 177 cm x 136 cm (69¾″ x 53½″).

Materials Required:
Linen: 1.85 m (2 yds), 150 cm (60″) wide. White cotton braid: 0.5 cm (¼″) wide, 62 m (68 yds).

Preparing the cloth
Cut out the cloth to the correct size, adding a 4 cm (1½″) hem allowance all around. Mark the horizontal and vertical center with lines of basting stitches. Onto tissue paper, trace 3 corner motifs and enough side motifs to form one short and one long side. Using the photograph as a guide, place the motifs along two sides of the cloth. When you have found the correct position, mark guide lines all around the cloth between which the design will run. Use basting stitches for these lines, following the grain of fabric. Check that the border fits into the other 2 sides correctly. Now transfer the motifs to the cloth with dressmaker's carbon paper.

Attaching the braid
Stitch on the braid with backstitch as shown on the right, following the lines of the design. In spite of the complicated appearance of the curving pattern, there are, in fact, only four interlocking lines and you begin a new length of braid only four times. Simply follow through with a long strip until you come back to where you started.
Sew two straight lines of braid 1 cm (⅜″) apart 2 cm (¾″) from the inner and outer edges of the pattern. These lines can be stitched on by machine.

Finishing
Turn under the hem twice, mitering the corners, and sew in place. Two more strips of braid can be sewn around the outer edges of the cloth, but additional braid will be required.

◀ The interlaced lines of braid make a graceful border pattern.

How-to

Embroidery with braid

For this kind of decoration, choose any braid which is flexible enough to apply in curved lines.

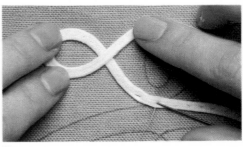

1 Place the braid along the lines of the design and sew it on with small, widely-spaced backstitches. Do not stretch the braid or the fabric will pucker.

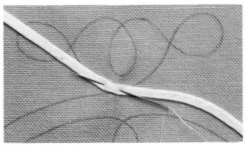

2 On the small, tight curves, it is advisable to shape the braid along the line first, holding it down flat with your fingers as you work.

3 Sew the beginning and end of the braid together, keeping them flat. Make sure that they meet where they will be covered by another line of braid.

Graceful tablecloth border design

The flowing lines of this design make an elegant border for a table cloth. The traced lines are covered with narrow braid which is sewn on with small backstitches.

Two joined side repeats

Corner motif with two side repeats ▶

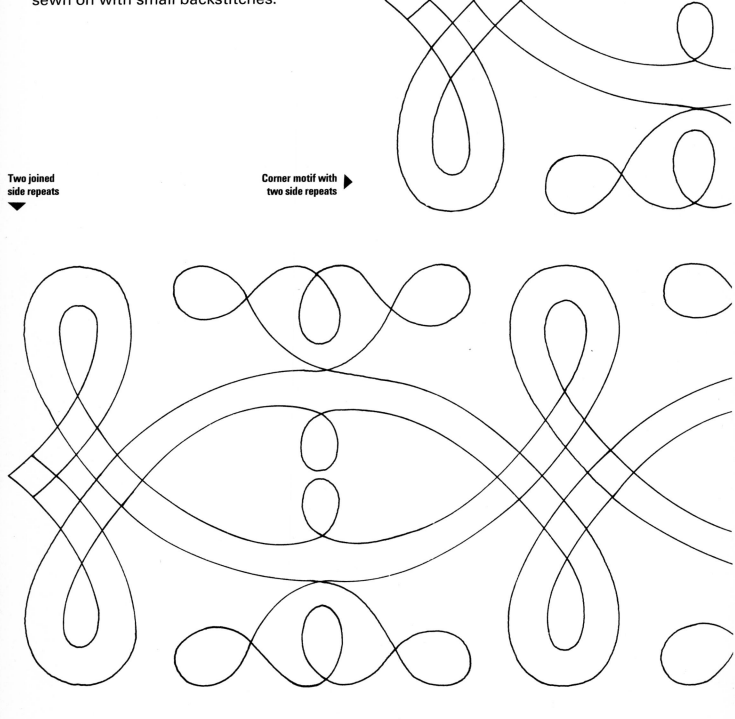

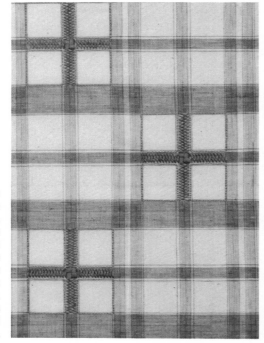

Here is a detail of the embroidered tablecloth. The squares are filled in with cross-stitch and the center of the wide stripes with a row of zigzag stitch.

This variation is worked on the same checked pattern. The large squares are outlined with backstitch, while the centers are filled in with satin stitch. The cross lines are in closed herringbone stitch.

This is one way to decorate striped fabric. Two rows of blanket stitch are worked opposite each other along the stripes and then laced with a contrasting thread.

Pick out the patterns

Try a new approach to an embroidered tablecloth by highlighting certain areas of patterned fabric. The cloth shown here measures 156 cm x 186 cm (61½″ x 73½″), with an invisible seam down the center of one of the embroidered stripes. The stitches are shown in close-up in the How-to.

Interlaced zigzag stitch, Closed herringbone stitch, Interlaced blanket stitch

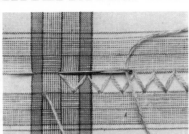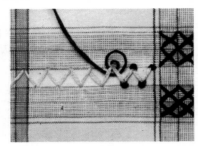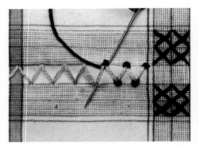

To work each side of the **zigzag stitch,** insert the needle back to where the previous stitch ended, alternately at top and bottom. The

zigzag row is interlaced with a contrasting thread. Bring the needle out to the left of the point, wrap the thread twice around both arms

of the zigzag and insert on the right of the point. Repeat on the lower point and continue in the same way across the zigzag row.

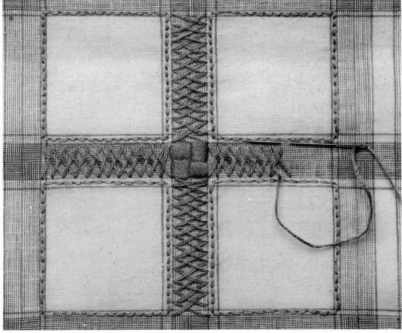

Closed herringbone stitch gives a firm, close line of embroidery. Take the thread to the right from bottom to top. Make a small stitch to the left, bringing the needle out at the top of the previous stitch. Take the thread to the bottom and make a small stitch to the left to the base of the previous stitch. Repeat.

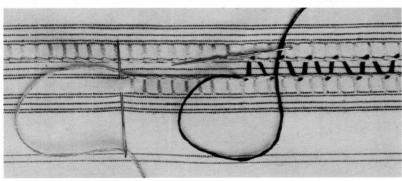

For interlaced blanket stitch, first work 2 rows of blanket stitch opposite each other and with the loops facing. Then lace in the contrasting thread by inserting the needle through every other stitch in staggered formation. Draw the thread through loosely.

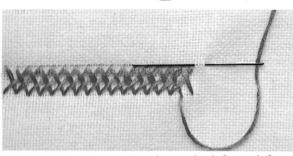

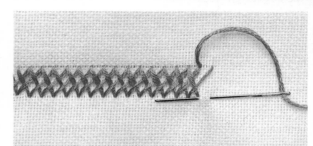

Closed herringbone stitch is worked from left to right, by taking backstitches alternately at top and bottom. No spaces are left between the stitches. On the back of the fabric will be two rows of backstitch.

Shadow work is only effective on transparent fabrics. Mark outlines with running stitch. Fill in from the wrong side with closed herringbone stitch. On the right side it will appear as an outlined shadow.

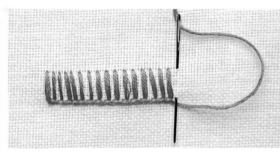

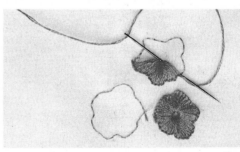

Buttonhole or close blanket stitch worked from left to right. Keep the thread under the needle tip as you bring it out and a looped edge will be formed. For a center hole, work in a circle around center point.

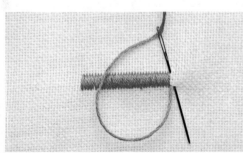

Overcasting stitch is a narrow satin stitch. In eyelet hole embroidery, outline the design with running stitch, then cut into the fabric, turning and catching it under with overcasting stitches. Trim the edges.

Hemstitch is now rarely used in its
original form to simply sew
a hem. Instead, it is used as
a decorative stitch
in drawn-thread embroidery.

Drawnwork to enhance beautiful linens

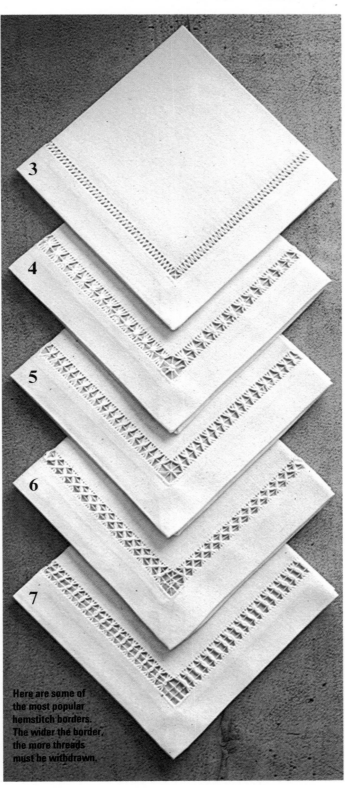

Here are some of the most popular hemstitch borders. The wider the border, the more threads must be withdrawn.

Hemstitch and needle-weaving are the two techniques used in drawnwork.

It gives a distinctive decorative finish to table linens, clothes, and accessories.

Size: The finished size of the place mats is 30 x 40 cm (11¾″ x 15¾″). The napkins are 30 cm (11¾″) square. Cut out the pieces along the grain of the fabric to measure 40 x 50 cm (15¾″ x 19¾″) and 40 cm (15¾″) square respectively. This includes twice the 2.5 cm (1″) hem allowance to make a double turning. The first turning can be slightly narrower if necessary.

Materials Required: Medium-weight even-weave linen. White stranded embroidery cotton (use 4 strands or match the thickness of the linen threads).

Drawing the threads

Mark the position of the hem and the drawn-thread areas on the wrong side of the fabric with pins or fine pencil lines. The outer drawn threads will be about 7.5 cm (3″) in from the edges. The width of the drawn-thread areas on Nos. 1–3 is 0.5 cm (¼″), on Nos. 4–7, 1 cm (⅜″).

Draw out the threads. On the place mats, the drawn threads cross at the corners and extend to the edges of the fabric, so draw the threads from the outside inward. On the napkins and inside the place mats, where the drawn threads do not extend to the edges, cut the outer thread in the middle and draw out to both sides as far as the marks. Continue withdrawing threads until the open area is the required width. Either weave in the ends of the threads invisibly or cut off the fabric thread ends and finish the edges with buttonhole or overcasting stitch. Miter the corners; turn under the hem.

Embroidering

Work hemstitch along the top and bottom of the drawn-thread areas. In Nos. 2 and 3, group four threads together; for the rest, group three threads together. In No. 1 use ladder hemstitch. The squares inside the border are worked in overcast bars. No. 2 is overcast ladder hemstitch. No. 3 is zigzag hemstitch. For Nos. 4–7, the thread groups are tied in a decorative way. Three groups are connected in Nos. 5 and 7, four in Nos. 4 and 6.

Fill in the empty corners on the narrow designs with crossed threads. The larger corners are filled in with several crossed threads in a design matching the style of the work. Do not pull these threads too tight.

Making the hem

Turn under the hem before working the outer row of hemstitch. The hem edge is then caught in with the stitching. On the place mats, work the small designs inside the main border areas, then work the border and the hem. At the corners, the hemstitching or overcasting will be worked over three layers of fabric.

Drawn-thread embroidery

Plain hemstitch

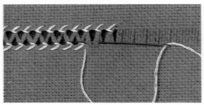

1 Work from left to right on the wrong side of the fabric. Pass the needle from right to left behind the required number of threads.

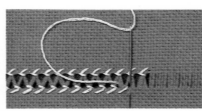

2 Insert the needle at the same point, going two fabric threads down. For ladder hemstitch, repeat on the other side with the same groups.

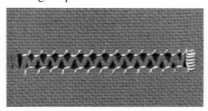

3 Zigzag hemstitch (right side): work over an even number of threads. On opposite side, each group is made up of $\frac{1}{2}$ the threads from two adjacent groups.

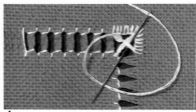

4 Corners are finished with close buttonhole stitch. To fill corners, stretch the thread over crosswise several times and buttonhole-stitch over middle to form a cross.

Hemstitch variations

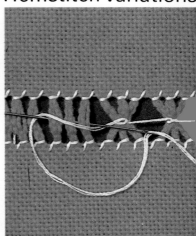

1 Gather several groups of threads together and fasten them with a slip knot. To do this, form a loop with the thread and, with the needle above the loop, pass it behind the groups. Bring it out inside the loop and pull the thread carefully to tighten the knot so that the distance between the groups is equal. You can work this stitch from either side of the fabric.

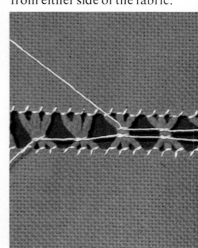

2 Work two rows of slip knots in the same way. Work from right to left and from either side of the fabric at equal intervals. Napkin border No. 7 is worked with this decorative stitch.

Mark the length and width of the drawn-thread areas on the wrong side of the fabric. Draw out the threads, then embroider the remaining threads with hemstitch variations.

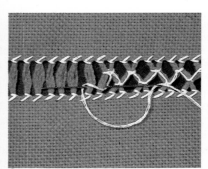

3a For a double zigzag effect, thread groups are joined in a staggered formation. Because the working thread runs from one slip knot to another, the stitches must be worked from the wrong side. Pass the needle behind two thread groups about one third up from the base to begin this stitch.

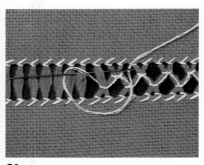

3b Loop the thread up and around to form another slip knot, passing the needle behind the last group and the next group along, about two thirds up from the base. Pull the knot tight.

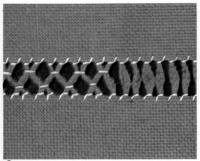

3c The double zigzag as seen from the right side of the fabric.

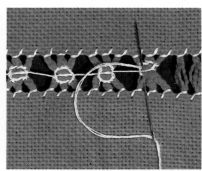

4 Join several groups of threads with slip stitches, then work small circles in the center in stem stitch or backstitch.

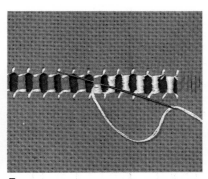

5 The groups of threads in ladder hemstitch can be closely overcast to form wrapped bars.

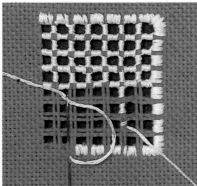

6 For a grid design, first overcast the raw edges closely. Then overcast the remaining horizontal and vertical threads firmly to form wrapped bars, giving a trellis effect.

Forming hem and corners

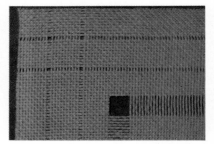

1 Allow three times the required width of the hem (for the double turning and the front). Mark the fold lines on heavy linen by drawing a thread along them and on fine linen with a pencil line. Withdraw the threads.

2 To miter the corners neatly, fold them in once so that the marked lines meet. Cut off the corner points evenly at the inner turning line.

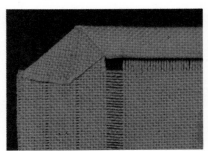

3 Now turn the hem under twice and baste it in place. Slip-stitch the mitered corners together. Catch in the edges of the hem as you work the hemstitch.

Specially Norwegian

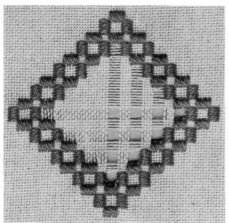

First, embroider the 3 rows of the outer Diamond, then the 2 rows of the inner one (the surround of the openwork Diamond) in vertical and horizontal satin stitch blocks, counting the threads as on graph. The last stitch of one satin block and the first stitch of the next one emerge from the same point. Begin with the upper satin stitch block and continue working clockwise. After finishing Diamond motifs, fabric threads for openwork are withdrawn (green lines on chart). Cut threads close to embroidery.

Weave around remaining loose threads. On each bar of 4 fabric threads, weave under and over two pairs of threads alternately, ie. insert needle into center and draw out alternately in one direction, then the other. Do not work too tightly. Working in steps, begin darning at upper horizontal thread bar, moving diagonally to the left-hand corner, then back to right-hand corner. Work all thread bars of the Diamond openwork in this way to form a lattice pattern.

Size: 116 cm x 46 cm ($45\frac{5}{8}$" x 18").
Materials Required: White even-weave fabric, 10 threads to 1 cm (26 threads to 1"): 0.70 m ($\frac{3}{4}$ yd), 140 cm (54") wide. Pearl Cotton No. 5: 12 skeins white. Embroidery hoop.

Making the runner

Trim fabric along straight of grain and finish edges. Use a hoop except when withdrawing threads and weaving bars. Begin the embroidery with the first Diamond at center of one of narrow ends, 9 cm ($3\frac{1}{2}$") from fabric edge. Start at upper edge of graph pattern and work around clockwise. On the graph, $\frac{1}{4}$ of the Diamond with its corners is given; work the other parts of the Diamond as a mirror image. Each grid line of the graph pattern represents 1 fabric thread. The diagonal lines represent lines of backstitch, while the green lines represent the fabric threads which are drawn out later to form the openwork diamonds (see photograph on far left). First, embroider 7 Diamonds with a space of 4 fabric threads between each. Complete all the Diamonds, then draw out the threads of the inner openwork Diamonds and weave the remaining threads to form bars (see photograph on near left). Embroider 4 backstitch rows parallel to the long sides, 4 fabric threads away from the Diamonds and 2 threads closer to the ends than the Diamonds. Begin with 2 staggered rows of backstitch over 4 fabric threads in length and 2 fabric threads apart. Begin and end the rows 2 threads further out than the Diamonds. Then work another 2 rows of backstitch, staggering the stitches in the 2nd row only. Next, work the Zigzag Edging in satin stitch and backstitch, 8 fabric threads away from the backstitch rows and using the section on the graph as a guide. Begin and end the same distance from the edge as the backstitch. Finally, work the outer edge in backstitch, beginning at center of short sides. On short sides, it is 4 fabric threads from the Diamonds and 2 fabric threads from Zigzag Edging. On long sides, it is 9 cm ($3\frac{1}{2}$") from outer points of Zigzag Edging. Count 2 fabric threads away from the backstitching and draw out 1 thread all around; weave in at the corners. For hem, measure out 6 cm ($2\frac{1}{4}$"). trim along straight thread. Sew under 2 cm ($\frac{3}{4}$") twice, mitering corners.

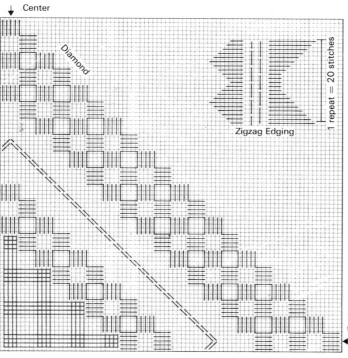

Counted-thread pattern. Graph shows $\frac{1}{4}$ Diamond with corners and 1 repeat pattern of the Zigzag Edging. The fine grid lines represent fabric threads. The thick lines are the embroidery stitches. The green lines are the fabric threads which are later drawn out of the openwork diamonds.

Traditional white embroidery
on white fabric is very
elegant, as our table runner
in Hardanger work illustrates.
This beautiful old embroidery
technique originated in
Norway and is called after
the fjord of the same name.

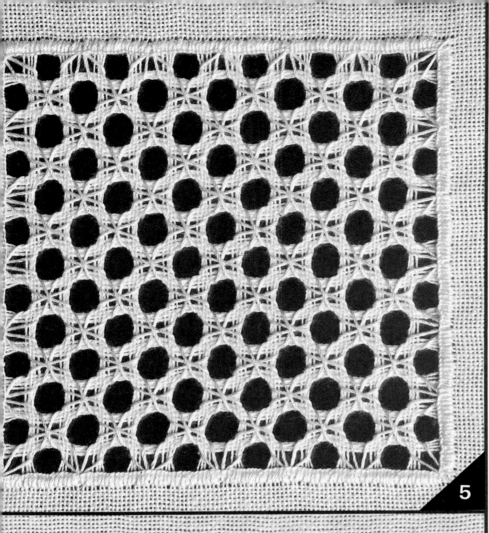

5

Drawn-thread work fillings
Space fillers

Beautiful delicate patterns like the ones shown here are produced by drawing threads from an even-weave fabric and then filling in the spaces in different ways. Most effective in white on white, these fillings make fine inserts for table and bed linen. They require considerable patience to work, but the end result is worth every moment spent on the embroidery.

On patterns **1** to **4**, only horizontal threads are withdrawn. Before beginning the filling embroidery, the long sides are finished with hem stitching.

For Patterns **1** and **3**, group every 2 woven threads and insert needle under 4 woven threads of fabric.

On Pattern **2**, group every 4 threads and insert needle under 4 woven threads of the fabric.

On Pattern **4**, group every 2 threads and insert the needle under 2 woven threads of the fabric.

On Patterns **5** and **6**, both lengthwise and crosswise threads are drawn and all sides are finished with buttonhole stitch. On the following pages, we show you how to work the drawn-thread patterns.

6

Working the patterns

For a base, use an even-weave fabric from which threads can easily be withdrawn. It is important that the warp and weft threads are of equal thickness. Linen or a cotton/linen blend is most suitable.

These patterns have been worked in two weights of pearl cotton.

Draw out the numbers of threads given. Do not cut them off at the edge; leave about 2.5 cm (1") to fold to the wrong side and secure with backstitches. Place backstitch line 2 threads from the edge, working over 2 threads at a time with fine pearl cotton.

Fasten the cotton with a few backstitches at the beginning rather than with a knot. When the filling is complete, finish the sides with a row of buttonhole stitch. The cut threads can now be trimmed.

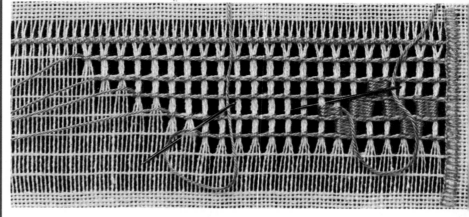

Pattern 1: Drawing threads: Draw 4 horizontal threads and leave 1 alternately 8 times, then draw another 4 threads. The vertical threads are grouped together with twisted chain stitch using fine pearl cotton.

Twisted chain stitch: Place working strand in a loop over threads to be bunched. Take needle to back of work at upper right hand, insert needle under required number of threads and bring out inside the loop (see needle on left). Pull strand taut. On the 2 outer rows, bunch every 2 threads together; on all other rows, bunch every 4 threads.

Between rows 4 and 5, weave together 2 groups of threads to fill in a square (see needle on right). Thicker pearl cotton is used for this. Next, fill in the square on the left in the row below, then the next square up to the left, and so on in a zigzag.

Pattern 2: Draw threads as for pattern 4. All twisted chain rows are worked over every 4 threads using fine pearl cotton. The Greek key design is woven into the resulting net, using thicker pearl cotton. For the long horizontal lines, weave all the squares in one continuous line (center needle). For the shorter vertical lines, work over 2 squares to the required height (needle on right). This technique is simple, but effective. When starting a new strand, fasten it with a few stitches at the back; do not knot.

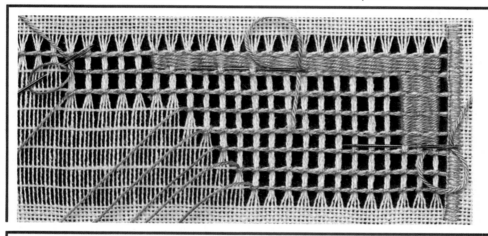

on left). Then, with thicker pearl cotton, work the woven bars in the center, securing them as follows: First fasten the cotton at top right of central area, take needle diagonally down behind the 1st lower 4-thread group and back again to the beginning. Weave around these 2 connecting threads from top to bottom. Emerge in front of the left-hand lower 4-thread group, take the needle diagonally up around the right-hand upper 4-thread group and back again. Weave around these connecting threads in the same way.

Finish the row of woven bars in the same way. Work a second row of bars over the first so that the 2 zigzag rows cross one another to form crosses.

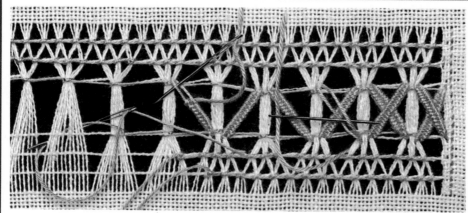

Pattern 3: Drawing threads: Draw 4 threads and leave 1 alternately 3 times. Then draw 12 threads. Leave 1 and draw 4 threads alternately 3 times. Work the twisted chain rows with fine pearl cotton. On the 2 outer rows, bunch every 4 threads; on the following 2 rows, stagger the groups of 4 threads. On the 2 center rows, bunch every 12 threads (see needle

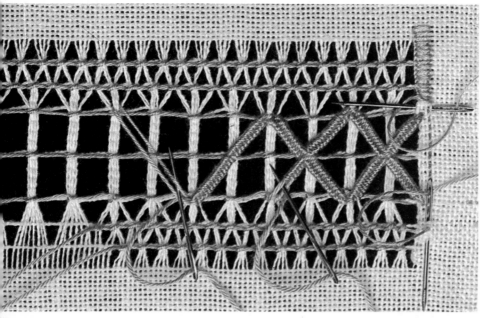

Pattern 4: Drawing threads: Draw 4 threads and leave 1 alternately 3 times. Then draw 9 threads twice, leaving 1 in between. Then leave 1 thread and draw 4 alternately 3 times. Work twisted chain rows with fine pearl cotton. On the 2 outer rows, bunch every 4 threads, on the 2 following rows, stagger the groups of 4 threads. In the center 3 rows, bunch every 8 threads, dividing every 2nd group of the previous row. The woven bars are worked with thicker pearl cotton over the 3 center twisted chain rows as for Pattern 3. The bars are attached to the embroidery thread of the middle twisted chain row so that they do not come away from the background. They are joined at the top and bottom to the center 4-thread group.

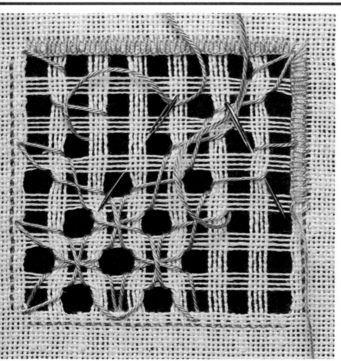

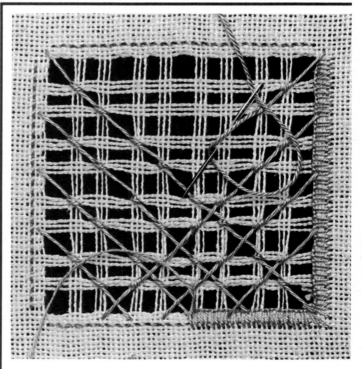

Pattern 5: Whatever the size of the square, the number of threads must be divisible by 8, plus 4 left over. Horizontally and vertically, draw 4 threads and leave 4 threads alternately; finally draw 4 threads. Work the 4-thread grid with thicker pearl cotton as follows: Fasten cotton in upper right-hand corner and pass needle diagonally around each woven square down to lower left-hand corner. Then insert needle into fabric corner and return (see needle on right). Work around every other woven square from upper right to lower left in this way. Then begin at upper left-hand corner and work the remaining woven squares from upper left to lower right, working diagonally around each woven square as before (see left needle), then work back up to upper left. The strands will cross in alternate spaces of the drawn-thread grid (see finished pattern in lower left corner).

Pattern 6: For this pattern, the number of threads must be divisible by 12, plus 4 left over. Horizontally and vertically, * draw 4 threads, leave 3, draw 2, leave 3; repeat from *, finally, draw 4 threads. With thicker pearl cotton, make a twisted chain stitch around each woven square as shown in the photograph above. Begin at top left-hand corner and work to lower right-hand corner. Work all other rows which begin at the top and left edge in the same way, always beginning in the corner of a large space and skipping the small spaces. Then work diagonally from right to left in the same way, beginning in the corner of the large spaces on the top and right edge. Begin and end all threads at the edge. Fasten off threads lightly: they will be secured firmly when the edge is finished with buttonhole stitch. Work the buttonhole stitch edge with finer pearl cotton.

In cut work

Heirloom embroidery

A fine tablecloth worthy of the true connoisseur of embroidery. This form of cut work is also called Richelieu embroidery after Cardinal Richelieu, Minister to King Louis XIII of France.

Size: 125 cm (49") square.
Materials Required:
Stranded embroidery cotton: 3 skeins white. White linen: 140 cm (54") wide, 1.90 m ($2\frac{1}{8}$ yd).

Making the cloth

Cut a 110 cm (43") square; the rest is for the border. Trace and transfer the motifs onto the fabric, positioning them 7 cm ($2\frac{3}{4}$") from the edges. Center the main motif on each side, placing the pointed motif at the corners and the linking motifs in between.

Work the preliminary outline stitches and the bars (including the stitches over the bars) with one strand of cotton. Cover the outlines with closely worked buttonhole stitch, using two strands of cotton. Finally, cut out the center of the motifs with bars and the large oval in the main motif.

Making the border

Cut four strips, 18 cm (7") wide, the length of the cloth plus 18 cm (7") for the corners. Stitch the strips onto the cloth, right sides together, with a 1 cm ($\frac{3}{8}$") seam allowance. Miter the corners (see Mitering How-to). Fold the strips in half lengthwise, and finish on the wrong side of the cloth by turning under the raw edges and slip-stitching to the seam by hand.

Cut work

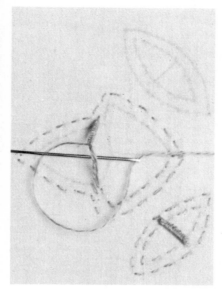

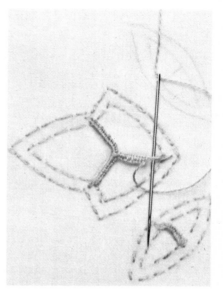

1 Outline the motifs with 2 rows of running stitches. On coming to the position for a bar, take the thread across the motif and back 3 times. Work the bar in buttonhole stitch to make it firm.

2 On completing the first bar, continue working running stitch to the next bar. Fasten this connecting bar to the center of the already completed bar and buttonhole stitch around it as before.

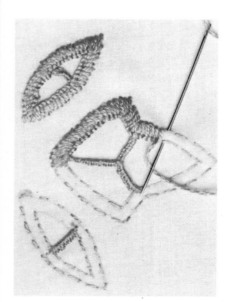

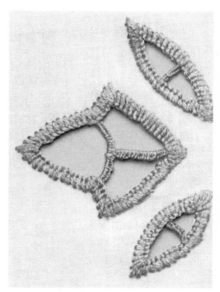

3 Embroider the outlines of the motifs with closely-worked buttonhole stitch, thus covering the preliminary running stitches.

4 After completing all the motifs around the cloth, cut away the fabric from the center very carefully with sharp-pointed scissors.

Join to main motif
at points A and B

A

B

Linking motif

Linking motif

A

C

Cut work border

B

Center the main motif on
the sides of the cloth

Embroider this delicate pattern around
the edge of a tablecloth and create
a beautiful family heirloom to treasure.

Work this motif
at the corners
of the cloth

The cross-stitch motifs on the following pages are used here to make a splendid border of flowers on a crisp white tablecloth to brighten up a corner of the dining room or living room. Choose an even-weave fabric such as cotton or linen on which you can easily count the threads. Use the photograph on the following pages as a guide to each motif for the positioning of the stitches and colors.

Size: The tablecloth illustrated is 132 cm (52″) square.

Materials Required: Stranded cotton: 3 skeins each in blue-green, pale grey-green, medium grey-green, pale lime green, dark lime green, grass green, pale green; 2 skeins each emerald green, pale blue-green dark green, olive, porcelain blue, pale blue, lilac, dark lilac, pink, red, orange, canary yellow, lemon yellow; 1 skein each dark grey-green, mid blue, dark blue, violet, turquoise, deep pink, dark russet, corn yellow. Even-weave cotton fabric, 9 threads to 1 cm (24 threads to 1″): 1.45 m (1⅝ yds), 150 cm (60″) wide.

Basic Stitch: Cross-stitch over 2 woven threads each in height and width. Work with only 4 strands of cotton.

Making the cloth

Cut out a 140 cm (55″) square of fabric on the straight of the grain. Mark a line 9 cm (3½″) from the cut edges with a colored basting thread. Begin by embroidering the small pansy corner motif, then follow the sequence of flowers as shown on the following pages. If you want to rearrange the motifs, work out their position before embroidering. When working cross-stitch, it is very important that the upper arms of the crosses all lie in the same direction. This gives a smooth overall appearance to the design; otherwise the result will look untidy.

Stitch each area of color separately and finish off the thread neatly afterward rather than carrying it across at the back. The reverse side of the cloth should look as neat as the front side.

To finish off the cloth, turn up a double hem 2 cm (¾″), mitering the corners. Stitch in place.

Everything's coming up flowers

We embroidered these delicate cross-stitch flowers on a tablecloth and you can see the stunning result on page 49. The flowers are shown here in actual size so that you can count the threads and follow the colors easily. On our repeat pattern for the cloth, the pansy, above left, is followed by the large yellow flower, below left. The sequence ends with the small yellow flower. The pansy, above right, is the corner motif.

Pride and glory

For the adventurous needlewoman, this masterpiece of a tablecloth offers a challenging, but satisfying project.

We have adapted this design so that you can embroider it yourself from the chart below.
A perfect result depends on careful counting.

Size: Approximately 137 cm x 109 cm (54" x 43").

Materials Required:
Stranded embroidery cotton: 10 skeins pink, 8 skeins beige, 7 skeins green, 5 skeins each red and grey, 3 skeins each black, dark blue and blue, 2 skeins each pale green and pale blue, 1 skein yellow. White even-weave fabric, 9 threads to 1 cm (24 threads to 1"): 1.80 m

Flower Motif Center   Half Repeat   Basket Motif Center

2 yds), 150 cm (59") wide.

Basic Stitch: Cross-stitch over 2 threads of weave each way, using half the strands of cotton.

Making the cloth

Trim the fabric to measure exactly 150 cm x 180 cm (59" x 72"). Work the Wide Border first, followed by the Upper and Lower Edge Motifs, then the Narrow Border, and the Stars.

To place the Wide Border, first mark the center of one long side, 15 cm (6") away from the edge of the fabric. Begin at the center mark with the center of the Flower Motif (at left-hand side of chart). Work the Half Repeat, including the center of the Basket Motif, then complete the other half of the Flower Motif on the other side of the center mark by following the chart in reverse without the 2 motif centers (126 crosses). Finish the right half of the side by working one more complete repeat and the Half Corner Motif. Finish the left half by working one more complete repeat and the Half Corner Motif in reverse. Continue to work around the cloth from right to left. Embroider the short sides with the Half Corner Motif, two complete repeats, and the Half Corner Motif in reverse. Embroider the other long side with the Half Corner Motif, three complete repeats, and the Half Corner Motif in reverse. Now embroider Upper and Lower Edge Motifs; begin at one corner and work around in one direction.

Then work the Narrow Border 56 threads up from the Upper Edge Motif on the long sides and 54 threads up on the short sides. On each side, begin centrally and at the center of a repeat pattern.

Finally work the Stars. For this, mark the exact center of the tablecloth with basting thread and work the first Star here. Continue in a lengthwise direction as follows: work another 4 Stars on each side of the center Star with 46 threads between each Star, i.e. 9 Stars in all. To left and right of this center row, work another two rows of Stars each side, each 46 threads apart, i.e. 5 rows in all. Then, between these, work more Star rows of 10 Stars each in a staggered formation. Work the Stars in a variety of colors such as dark blue with beige cross and red center or grey with pink cross and red center.

Finally, trim any excess fabric to give a 9 cm (3½") border all around, and turn in a small hem twice.

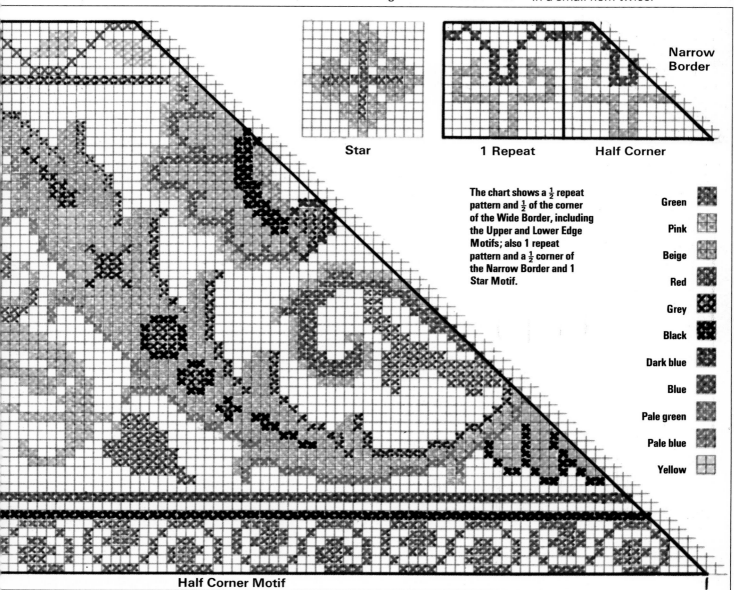

Star   **1 Repeat**   **Half Corner**   **Narrow Border**

The chart shows a ½ repeat pattern and ½ of the corner of the Wide Border, including the Upper and Lower Edge Motifs; also 1 repeat pattern and a ½ corner of the Narrow Border and 1 Star Motif.

Green
Pink
Beige
Red
Grey
Black
Dark blue
Blue
Pale green
Pale blue
Yellow

Half Corner Motif

Watch it grow stitch by stitch

For a country-look tablecloth,
embroider our tree and bird motifs.

Size: Approximately 106 cm (42¼")
square.

Materials Required: Cotton fabric:
90 cm (1 yd), 90 cm (36") wide in
cream; 110 cm (1¼ yds), 90 cm (36")
wide in green to match the embroidery. Stranded cotton: 1 skein each
of pale green, dark green, brown,
beige, blue-grey, blue; 2 skeins each
of medium green, pale brown.

Basic Stitch: Stem stitch worked
with undivided stranded cotton.

Working the embroidery

Trace and transfer a tree motif at
each corner of the cream fabric with
dressmaker's carbon paper. Place the
tree motif 2.5 – 3 cm (1" – 1¼") away
from the cut edges, with 8 bird motifs
scattered above it. Work all the
motifs in stem stitch. The tree trunk
is pale brown and brown, the foliage
pale green, medium green, and dark
green. For the birds, the outlines are
blue, the body beige and the wings
blue, or blue-grey and blue.

Making the cloth

From the green fabric, cut 4 strips
each 20 cm (8") wide, 108 cm
(43¼") long. Fold the strips in half
lengthwise. Miter the corners as
follows: on the wrong side, at the
beginning and end of each strip,
make a mark 11 cm (4⅜") in along
raw edge and 1 cm (⅜") in on folded
edge. Draw a diagonal line between
the marks. Repeat on other half of
each folded strip. Baste the 4 strips
together, right sides facing, along
the diagonal lines, then stitch them,
beginning 1 cm (⅜") from the raw
edges. Turn to the right side, then,
with right sides facing, stitch the
strips to the cloth with a 1 cm (⅜")
seam allowance. Fold half to the
back and sew down.

Here you can see how
the tree and little
birds are filled in
with stem stitch
in several shades
of each color

**Tree and
bird motifs**

Run, rabbit, run

Size: 130 cm (50″) square.

Materials Required: Stranded cotton: 1 skein each of light brown, dark brown, sea green, red, steel blue, dark burgundy; 2 skeins each of brown, golden yellow, leaf green. Fine linen: 1.40 m (1½ yds), 140 cm (54″) wide. Yellow soutache braid: 8.50 m (9¼ yds). Dressmaker's carbon paper.

Basic Stitches: Stem stitch, satin stitch, and French knots. Work all embroidery using 2 strands of the stranded cotton.

Working the embroidery

With basting thread, mark out a square in the center of the fabric. The square should measure at least 80 cm (31½″) square, but can be slightly larger if necessary to fit the dimensions of your table.

The motifs are given as actual-size patterns. Transfer duck motif to the fabric with dressmaker's carbon paper, placing it diagonally in each corner of the central square about 8 cm (3″) from the edges. Transfer large motif 1 cm (⅜″) above. Embroider all fine lines in stem stitch. Fill in areas such as grass, leaves, flowers, rabbits' ears, and chickens' claws in diagonal satin stitch. The eyes are French knots. Follow illustration for colors.

Finishing: Stitch soutache braid along the lines of basting thread to outline central square. Turn under 2.5 cm (1″) hem twice, mitering corners. Stitch soutache braid along hem seam.

The charming motifs on this tablecloth evoke all the freshness and delicacy of a spring day. They are worked in stem stitch, satin stitch, and French knots on fine linen.

Easter embroidery

For a delightful Easter tablecloth, transfer these animal motifs onto white linen and embroider them in simple stitches.

59

Here is the main motif – the hen – shown actual size. Trace the outlines from this photograph and transfer them to the fabric with dressmaker's carbon paper.

Set your Easter table with this gay appliqué cloth in bright springtime colors.

*

Size: The cloth measures 132 cm (52") square and has a center seam.

Materials Required:
Green linen, cotton, or linen mixture: 3 m (3¼ yds), 90 cm (36") wide.
Red braid: 5 m (5½ yds). Remnants of white and printed cotton fabrics. Bonding net or web for ironing-on motifs. Red fabric paint.

Making the cloth
Cut the fabric crosswise into two pieces. Stitch the center seam. Trim the cloth to measure 148 cm (58") square. Baste under an 8 cm (3") hem all around, mitering the corners. On the right side, stitch the braid over the hem stitching line. Trace the hen from the photograph above and transfer to the white fabric. Press the bonding net onto the back and cut out the shape exactly. Peel the backing off the bonding net when cool. Cut out the eggs measuring 6 cm (2½") in diameter from different patterned fabrics and prepare in the same way.

Arrange the hens and eggs along the edge of the cloth and pin in position. Then iron on the motifs one after the other, pressing down firmly with a hot iron. Stitch all around the outlines with a close zigzag machine stitch. Paint the hen's beak, comb, and wattles with red fabric paint.

For a larger or smaller cloth, rearrange motifs.

In colorful appliqué

Hen party

61

There will be sweet dreams for baby
with these whimsical dozing sheep
on the sheets and pillowcase.
With such enchanting companions,
you'll have no more trouble
getting the children to bed!

Sleepy-time sheep

A row of lovable woolly sheep make a delightful decoration for a child's sheets. The large sheep on the pillow even sports a monogram — an idea which will appeal to adults, too! You can also embroider these motifs onto clothes or other nursery furnishings.

Materials Required: Stranded cotton in pale pink, deep pink, pale blue, dark blue, and white. For the large motif: 1 skein pale blue, ½ skein each of the other colors. For the border: the same quantities.

Basic Stitch: Satin stitch worked with only 2 of the 6 strands in the needle.

Working the embroidery

Trace the motifs from the pattern and transfer to the fabric with dressmaker's carbon paper. Work the sheep in pale blue with white hooves; work ears and face in pale pink. Work the ground in pale pink. The flowers have pale pink and deep pink petals; the leaves and stems are 2 shades of blue.

Trace the required letters for your own monogram onto the fabric and embroider each letter in deep pink with a white border.

Sheep motifs for bed linen

Embroider these whimsical motifs onto
your child's sheets or anywhere else
in the nursery. Add initials for fun.

Wild goose chase

This embroidered picture, depicting the goose girl from the traditional fairy tale, would look charming on a nursery wall.

Size: 40 cm (15¾") wide x 28 cm (11") high.

Materials Required: Stranded cotton in the following colors: 1 skein each pink, blue, pale blue, slate blue, pale grey, grey, dark brown, yellow, red, orange, lime green, leaf green, dark green, olive. Piece of fine linen measuring 52 cm x 40 cm (20½" x 15¾"). 1 picture frame. Hardboard.

Basic Stitches: Stem stitch, satin stitch, and French knots worked with 2 strands.

Working the embroidery
Transfer the motif onto the center of the fabric with dressmaker's carbon paper. Work all outlines in stem stitch, wider lines in diagonal satin stitch, filled-in areas in satin stitch, and dots in French knots. Follow the illustration for colors.

Finishing
Press the embroidery lightly from the back under a damp cloth. Stretch the picture over a piece of hardboard cut to the size of the frame, lace it at the back with thread, and pull taut. Place the picture into the frame; secure at the back.

Create a wisp of a curtain

This curtain has a wonderfully light and
airy appearance. The
delicate embroidered border is worked in
drawn fabric stitches
onto loosely-woven cotton. Although it
needs a fair amount of patience and
good eyesight, the end result is breathtaking.

Size: Width about 110 cm (43″).
Materials Required: For the two curtains in the width given, use stranded embroidery cotton in the following colors and quantities: 6 skeins olive, 4 skeins apricot, 3 skeins each yellow, lilac, lime green, turquoise, 2 skeins rose, 1 skein green. Metallic gold thread: 1 skein. Loosely-woven cotton in natural color: 112 cm (45″) wide, in required length, plus 15 cm (6″) for hems.

Preparing the fabric

Rinse the fabric in clear water, let it dry, and iron it.

Trace and transfer the lower border first 15 cm (6″) above the fabric edge, repeating as many times as necessary and adding the border ends at the side edges.

Transfer the large motifs 3 cm (1⅛″) above the border, about 9 cm (3½″) apart. Alternate the Tree of Life with the other two motifs.

Transfer the small motifs in between the large ones and the narrow border 6 cm (2½″) above the large motifs.

Working the embroidery

The basic stitches are four-sided stitch used as a surface stitch, four-sided stitch used as a drawn fabric stitch, honeycomb stitch, satin stitch, and stem stitch, with some cross-stitch. Use 4 strands of stranded cotton in the needle. The four-sided drawn fabric stitch is worked over 3 to 4 threads of the fabric.

Making the curtain

Turn up a 5 cm (2″) hem twice and stitch close to the bottom edge of the wide border. Hem top and side edges. Steam the hems and the embroidery carefully on the right side.

Narrow Border: embroider the vine in stem stitch. The trefoils are outlined with stem stitch and the drawn fabric areas are filled in with four-sided stitch. Use olive for the vine, and turquoise with lilac or turquoise with apricot for the trefoils.

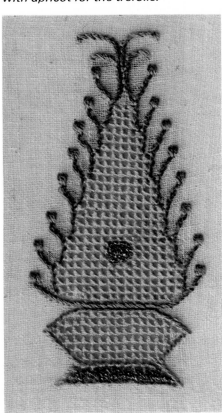

Tree of Life: the outlines are worked in stem stitch and the dots in satin stitch. The drawn fabric areas are then filled in with four-sided stitch to form an openwork trellis effect. The base is worked in satin stitch and the circle in the center in satin and stem stitch using gold thread. Colors: lilac, rose, yellow, and green.

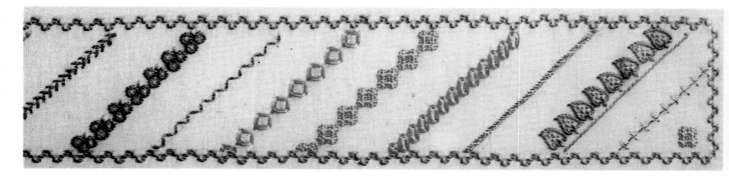

Wide Border: *work the outline first in honeycomb stitch using olive stranded cotton, then work the slanting lines.*

Staggered Line: *work half four-sided stitch in gold thread.*

Trefoils: *the outlines are worked in stem stitch in turquoise and the drawn fabric areas are filled in with four-sided stitch in apricot.*

Stepped Lines: *work these in half four-sided stitch in gold thread.*

Squares: *the outer squares are worked in lime green four-sided stitch, the inner ones in apricot.*

Four-flower Squares: *the outline is worked in stem stitch in rose, then filled in with four-sided stitch in lime green.*

Rectangles: *work the outlines in apricot four-sided stitch with the vertical stitches double the length of the horizontal stitches. Fill in with satin stitch in lilac.*

Gold Stripe: *work horizontal satin stitch using gold thread.*

Leaf Line: *the diagonal line is yellow stem stitch; the leaf outline is green stem stitch filled in with four-sided stitch in yellow.*

Border Ends: *embroider the four-flower square as above and the line next to it in gold-thread cross-stitch.*

Motif with Diamonds: *the outlines are worked in stem stitch, the drawn fabric areas in four-sided stitch, and the lines at the diamond points are straight stitches. The gold stripes are worked in satin stitch and the gold crosses inside the flowers are large cross-stitches. The colors used are lime green, lilac, and apricot.*

Small Motifs: *the outlines are worked in stem stitch and the inner areas in four-sided stitch. The colors are rose with lime green, green with yellow, and lilac with apricot.*

Clover Motif: *the outlines are worked in stem stitch and the drawn fabric areas in four-sided stitch. The gold stripe is worked in satin stitch and the gold crosses inside the clover leaves can be worked as cross-stitches or four straight stitches. The colors used are lime green, olive, apricot, rose, and turquoise.*

Four-sided stitch

Four-sided stitch can be varied in several ways to produce very different effects. It can be used as a border pattern or as a filling stitch. It can also be worked as a surface or a drawn fabric stitch.

1a Four-sided stitch as a surface stitch: If using an even-weave fabric, work over 3 or 4 threads for each stitch, otherwise follow the transferred outline. Insert the needle vertically down and bring it out again diagonally to to the left. The horizontal and vertical stitch length should always be the same.

1b Insert the needle back into the top of the first stitch and bring it out diagonally down to the left. The two stitches which have now been worked form two sides of a square.

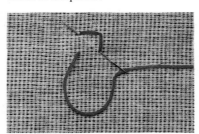

1c Insert the needle into the base of the first stitch, bringing it out diagonally up to the left. Repeat from 1a.

2 Four-sided stitch worked diagonally: First follow the steps shown in 1a to 1c. When completing the fourth side of the square, bring the needle out twice the length of one stitch to the right. This is the starting point for the next stitch.

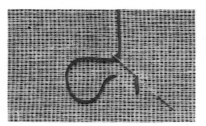

3a Half four-sided stitch worked diagonally: Begin working as described in 1a. Then insert the needle back into the top of the first stitch and bring it out diagonally down to the right. Make sure the horizontal and vertical stitches are equal.

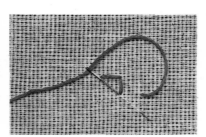

3b Insert the needle to the base of the first stitch and bring it out diagonally down to the right, below the last thread.

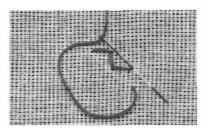

3c Continue working alternate horizontal and vertical stitches to form a stepped line.

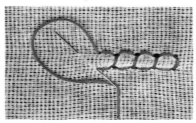

4 Four-sided stitch as a drawn fabric stitch: This is worked in the same way as 1a–1c, but the thread should be pulled firmly after each stitch so that the fabric threads are drawn apart making an openwork pattern. This is used as a filler stitch.

5 Honeycomb stitch: Only the first step is shown here, where the needle is inserted into the fabric and brought out horizontally to the left. Second step: bring the needle back and make another stitch in the same place. Then move up or down and work a double horizontal stitch.

Embroider a border

Add a decorative border to simple curtains. This embroidery is stunning on light and airy fabrics such as loosely-woven cotton. Traditional motifs such as the Tree of Life are worked in drawn fabric stitches in delicate colors.

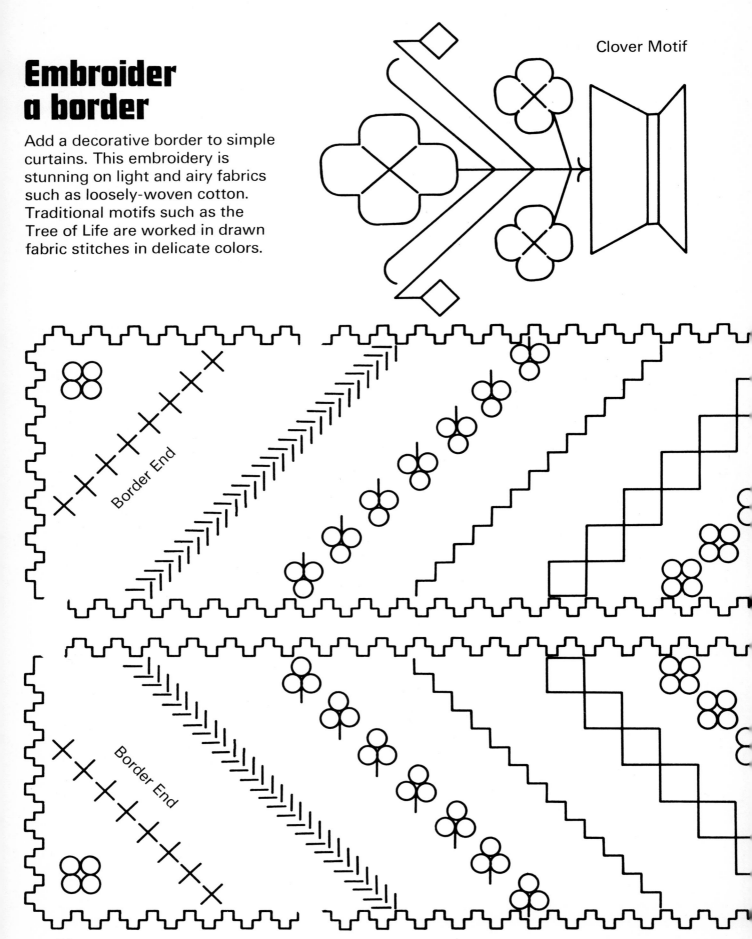

Clover Motif

Border End

Border End

Motif with Diamonds

Narrow Border

Small Motifs

Left Curtain

Right Curtain

Repeat border
to fit width of curtain

Tree of Life
Motif

Cushions for cat lovers

Cat lovers will be enchanted by this cushion. The cat, worked in loops of tapestry yarn on velvet, has three-dimensional fur. On the left is a variation in pinks on burgur...

Embroidered on velvet

Size: Velvet cushion is 40 cm (16″) square.

Materials Required:

Tapestry yarn in the following colors and quantities:

Pink cat: 3 skeins each of 3 medium rose colors, 4 skeins deep rose, 5 skeins pale pink.

Green cat: 1 skein olive, 2 skeins each pale green and dark olive, 4 skeins moss green, 5 skeins lime.

Both: Small amounts of shiny embroidery threads in harmonizing colors for the cat's bow. 2 stuffed-toy eyes. Olive or burgundy velvet: 45 x 90 cm (18″ x 36″). Cushion: 40 cm (16″) square. Organza: 45 cm (18″) square. Embroidery frame.

Working the embroidery

Cut the velvet into 2 pieces measuring 44 cm (17½″) square. Trace the cat and transfer onto the organza with dressmaker's carbon paper, adding the tip of the tail at the back of the cat. Baste the organza to the front of one of the squares of velvet with closely-spaced parallel lines.

Embroider the separate areas of the cat in loop stitch in different shades, changing the direction of the stitches according to the photograph on the right. When the embroidery is complete, remove the basting and carefully cut away the excess organza. Sew on the glass eyes.

Making the cushion

Place the two squares of velvet together, right sides facing, and stitch around three sides. Turn to right side. Insert the cushion and slip-stitch the opening closed.

Attach tail
to cat body

Cat motif in loop stitch

Attach tail here

Loop stitch

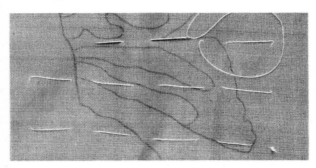

1 Baste the organza with the transferred motif onto the right side of the velvet.

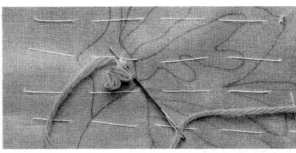

2 Work the loops in rows. Insert the needle and bring it out about 3–4 mm ($\frac{1}{8}$″) away.

3 Let the yarn form upstanding loops of equal height. Work the rows close together, changing direction where necessary.

4 Work with an embroidery frame to prevent the organza from puckering. When the embroidery is complete, remove the basting and cut away the excess organza.

A pretty motif for your pullover
Pick a glossy leaf

Spice up a plain pullover with an embroidered motif. The leaf shown here is worked in a shiny embroidery thread on fluffy angora for a pleasing contrast of textures.

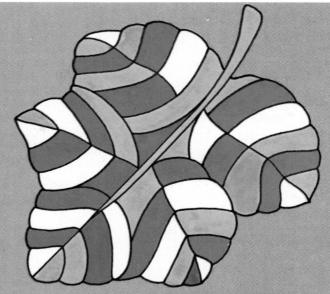

Materials Required:
Pearl cotton or stranded cotton in dark green, pale green, and white. Piece of white tissue paper. Thread.

Basic Pattern: Satin stitch worked with undivided thread.

Tracing the motif
Trace the motif shown above onto white tissue paper. Cut roughly around the shape and baste to the pullover just below the shoulder. Work small running stitches around the lines of the motif with sewing thread used double. Pull away the tissue paper carefully, leaving the running-stitch outline.

Working the motif
Now embroider the leaves in two shades of green and white in satin stitch, placing the colors as shown in the illustration. Cover the running stitches as you work. Work the satin stitch straight up and down between the lines of each color area. Embroider the thicker end of the stem in satin stitch and the narrow part between the leaves in stem stitch in pale green.
The leaves would also look effective on the pocket of a cardigan or on a T-shirt.

Embroidery on a knitted tank top

Fishing for compliments

Buy a plain
tank top and
embroider it
for fun with
this cheerful
angler motif.

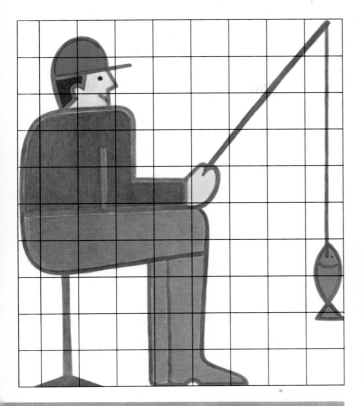

▲ Enlarging the motif on white paper:
Man's tank top: For every square on the diagram, draw a square measuring 2.5 cm x 2.5 cm (1″ x 1″) onto the paper. Boy's tank top: Draw squares measuring 2 cm x 2 cm (¾″ x ¾″). Transfer the outlines onto the new grid for the actual-size embroidery motif. Then trace the motif onto thin tissue paper.

Materials Required:

Tapestry yarn in the following colors and quantities. Man's tank top: 1 skein each light red (for cap and fish), beige (for face and hand), brown (for hair and eye), light brown (for trousers), orange (for boots), pale blue (for seat and outline); 2 skeins moss green (for pullover). Boy's tank top: 1 skein each scarlet (for cap, pullover, fish), black (for hair and eye), beige (for face and hand), blue (for trousers), orange (for boots), grey (for seat and outline).

Working the embroidery

Baste the tissue paper to the tank top and outline the motif with running stitches. Tear the paper away carefully, leaving the running stitch outline to indicate the areas to embroider.
Work the motif in Swiss darning or duplicate stitch as shown in the photographs on the right. Finally, outline the figure in stem stitch. Work 2 rows of stem stitch for the fishing rod, 1 row for the line.

How-to

Filling stitches

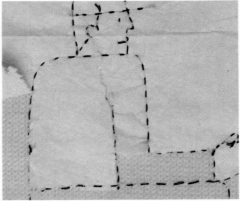

First outline the motif in running stitch over the tissue paper. Tear the paper away carefully from the motif.

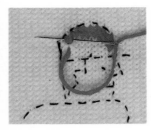

Embroider each part separately. First follow the outline with ordinary small Swiss darning or duplicate stitches.

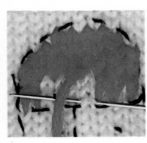

Continue by filling in areas with long Swiss darning or duplicate stitches worked over several vertical rows.

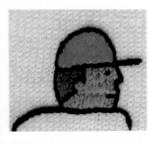

To finish off, work outlines in stem stitch, following the contours. Make a French knot for the eye.

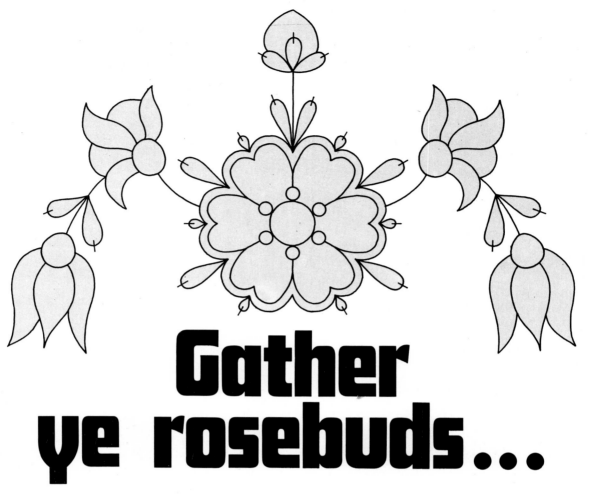

Gather ye rosebuds...

Cheer up your winter wardrobe with a little embroidery. Using easy stitches and a few skeins of tapestry yarn, you can turn a plain pullover into a really special garment. Choose subtle colors on a neutral background if you favor a sophisticated look; alternatively pick a zingy pullover and embroider it as brightly as possible.

Materials Required:
Tapestry yarn: for the blue pullover, 2 skeins each of dark red, bright red, and green; 1 skein of grey. For the red pullover, 2 skeins each of blue, green, and yellow; 1 skein each of red and white. White organza. Tapestry needle.

Working the embroidery
As the pattern cannot be transferred directly onto the pullover, trace it from

the outlines above and transfer it onto organza first, then baste this onto the pullover. The design can then be embroidered through the fabric and pullover together. When the embroidery is complete, the organza threads are drawn out with tweezers. The flowers and centers are worked in satin stitch, the stems in stem stitch, the leaves in lazy daisy stitch. The large flowers are then outlined in chain stitch. Follow the illustrations for colors.

◄ This version is bright and young-at-heart. The flower garlands are worked in vivid colors on a red pullover.

Here we chose a pale blue ►
pullover and
embroidered it in soft
rust and green shades
for an elegant look.

From oddments of yarn

Fresh as a daisy

Here is an idea for transforming your plain pullovers, cardigans, and tank tops into interesting and fashionable garments — and it takes very little time or trouble. Use oddments of embroidery cotton or yarn to make these small, colored flowers in lazy daisy stitch. Place them symmetrically or scatter them over the whole garment in a riot of color.

Materials Required: Small amounts of colored stranded cotton or tapestry yarn. Small beads. Tapestry needle.
Basic Stitch: Lazy daisy stitch.

Embroidering

Trace the outlines of the flowers onto tracing or tissue paper as circles and cut them out. Arrange the circles on the garment until they form a pleasing pattern and pin them in position. Decide on your color arrangement and note it on the appropriate circle. Choose toning colors or brightly contrasting ones. Now you can begin to embroider. Remove each circle as you come to it and work in the color specified.

When working the large

On this cardigan, large and small flowers in toning colors are placed in a symmetrical pattern on the shoulders and around the neckline. They are given actual-size on the right of the photograph.

flowers, take care not to pull up the loops of the lazy daisy stitch too tightly. The small flowers shown on the right have a bead sewn to the center of the petals, but a French knot could also be worked instead of a bead.

Important: Embroider each flower separately and finish off the yarn at the back. Never carry the yarn from flower to flower on the wrong side of the work, as this will pull the knitted fabric together and the loose strands may snag.

The small, brightly-colored flowers on this jacket give it a very feminine appeal. The different kinds of flowers are shown actual size on the right. Each one has a bead at the center of the petals. Position them at random with the front of the jacket closed.

Bulgarian beauty

Here's a real treat for embroiderers – a blouse with a traditional Bulgarian design. It has raglan sleeves and a widely-cut bodice. The motifs are in satin stitch and stem stitch.

Size: To fit bust sizes 88 cm–92 cm ($34\frac{1}{2}$″–36″).

Materials Required: Cotton: 2.10 m ($2\frac{1}{4}$ yds), 90 cm (36″) wide. Zipper: 20 cm (8″) long. 2 small buttons. Stranded cotton in the following colors and quantities: 3 skeins each yellow, white, and black; 2 skeins each blue and green; 1 skein red. Embroidery frame.

Cutting out: Place the pattern pieces on single fabric as shown on the cutting layout. Mark the outlines and lengthwise fold lines of collar and cuffs with basting. Add 2 cm ($\frac{3}{4}$″) for the hem; elsewhere add 1 cm ($\frac{3}{8}$″) seam allowance.

Positioning motifs: The embroidery motifs are given as an actual-size pattern. With dressmaker's carbon paper, transfer the front motif centrally, 7 cm ($2\frac{3}{4}$″) away from the neck edge. Transfer the 6 small tulip motifs onto the sleeve 3 cm (1″) from the neck edge; transfer the main sleeve motif 1 cm ($\frac{3}{8}$″) below this, then keep adding the small tulip motifs underneath to fill the space. Transfer the 3 upper tulips 1 cm ($\frac{3}{8}$″) below the motif on the front.

On the neckband and cuffs, transfer the border motifs to one lengthwise half only. For the cuffs, use the shorter flower border, for the neckband the longer one, making sure they are positioned centrally. The tips of the yellow heart-shaped flowers point toward the fold line on the neckband and to the cut edge on the cuffs.

Before embroidering: Finish all cut edges with zigzag stitch. So that the lower edge of sleeves, neckband, and cuffs can be stretched onto the frame, mount them onto remnants of fabric.

Embroidering: Fill in all areas with satin stitch and work all lines in stem stitch. Use half the strands of cotton.

After embroidering: Remove the extra pieces of fabric added for stretching into the frame.

Sewing: Join the center back seam up to beginning of zipper. Stitch side and sleeve seams, leaving sleeve open below arrows. Then stitch sleeves to front and back. Gather the neck edge to the length of the neckband and the lower sleeve edge to the cuff length (excluding underlap). Stitch the 2 narrow ends (center back) of the neckband and turn, then stitch one layer of fabric to the neck edge, right sides facing. Press seam toward the neckband, then turn in the seam allowance of the inside neckband and sew down along the seamline by hand. Stitch in the zipper invisibly at the back up to the upper edge of the neckband.

Finish the sleeve slit with a bias strip. Stitch and turn the cuffs and sew on in the same way as the neckband.

Make a looped fastening for the button on the overlap of the cuff. Sew the button into position on the underlap. Turn up and sew the hem.

Inch equivalents:		
	9 cm = $3\frac{1}{2}$″	19 cm = $7\frac{1}{2}$″
1.5 cm = $\frac{5}{8}$″	9.5 cm = $3\frac{3}{4}$″	22 cm = $8\frac{5}{8}$″
2 cm = $\frac{3}{4}$″	10 cm = $3\frac{7}{8}$″	23 cm = 9″
4 cm = $1\frac{5}{8}$″	11 cm = $4\frac{3}{8}$″	24 cm = $9\frac{1}{2}$″
4.5 cm = $1\frac{7}{8}$″	12 cm = $4\frac{3}{4}$″	28 cm = 11″
6 cm = $2\frac{3}{8}$″	13 cm = $5\frac{1}{8}$″	41 cm = $16\frac{1}{8}$″
6.5 cm = $2\frac{5}{8}$″	14 cm = $5\frac{1}{2}$″	42.5 cm = $16\frac{3}{4}$″
7.5 cm = 3″	16 cm = $6\frac{1}{4}$″	52 cm = $20\frac{1}{2}$″
8.5 cm = $3\frac{3}{8}$″	18.5 cm = $7\frac{1}{4}$″	61 cm = 24″

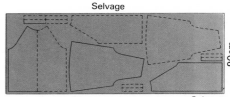

Cutting layout: Place pattern pieces on single fabric as shown above.

The pattern pieces for the blouse are shown below. Draw the pieces to the measurements on the diagram. The numbers are centimeters; inch equivalents are also given.

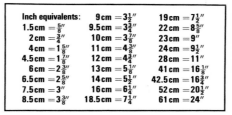

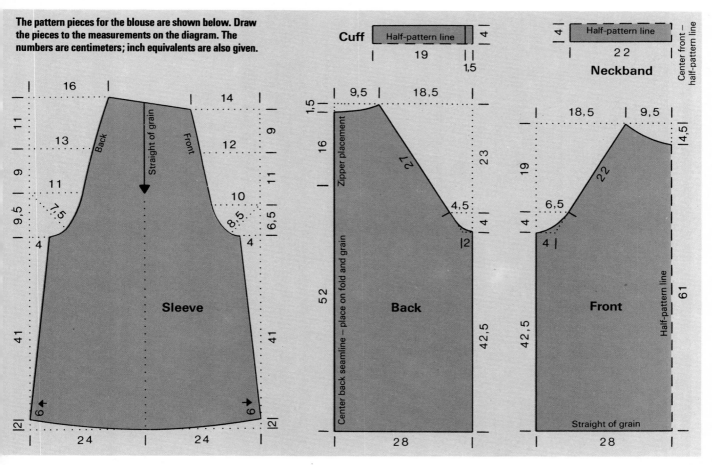

Sleeve

Embroidery for peasant blouse

This stunning embroidery is worked on the collar, cuffs, and bodice of a loose blouse.

A
Neckband — join
at points A

Cuff

Bodice front

Small tulip motifs

Size: To fit 84 cm–88 cm (33″–34½″) bust.

Materials Required: Bleached cotton: 1.40 m (1½ yds), 180 cm (72″) wide. Soft double-thread cross-stitch canvas, 20 holes to 5 cm (10 holes to 1″): 0.40 m (½ yd), 90 cm (36″) wide. Stranded embroidery cotton: 1 skein each of red, blue, green, yellow, and black. 4 small buttons.

Before cutting out: As the cotton may shrink, wash and iron it before cutting out.

Cutting out: See cutting layout. Enlarge pattern pieces from diagram. Front and back yoke and cuffs are embroidered. Place these pieces onto single fabric, cut front yoke and cuff twice, the back yoke once, adding 1 cm (⅜″) seam allowance all around. Cut off the rest of the fabric beyond these pieces. Mark the pattern outlines and fold lines with basting thread and cut out roughly.

Cut out the soft canvas to fit the embroidered parts of the yoke and cuffs. For front yoke, cut separate pieces for horizontal and vertical lines of embroidery. Baste into place on appropriate pattern piece.

Embroidering: Work over the canvas in cross-stitch with 2 strands of cotton, following design from chart. Part of the back yoke motif is also used for cuffs; work left corner with center motif onto right cuff and vice versa. On front yoke, work horizontal section of design first, then remove the canvas thread by thread. After this, work the vertical part; the 2 sections will not join at right angles as the yoke slopes outward toward the shoulder.

After embroidering: Draw out the canvas threads from the embroidered sections one by one. Cut out front and back yokes and cuffs exactly. With the remaining fabric doubled, cut out the rest of the pieces as on cutting layout, adding 1 cm (⅜″) seam allowance and 2 cm (¾″) for hem. For sleeve slits, cut 2 straight strips 4 cm (1½″) wide and 10 cm (4″) long.

Sewing: Join short center seam [1 cm (⅜″)] of front yoke. Press under facing along fold line. Gather front and back from center to * to width of relevant yoke, then stitch on. Finish cut edges together. Join side and shoulder seams. Work neckband as follows: stitch upper edge and short sides; turn. Stitch one layer of neckband to neck edge, right sides facing. Turn in the other seam allowance and sew on along seamline. Face sleeve slit with cut strip. Join sleeve seam. Gather sleeve top between * to 18.5 cm (7⅜″). Set in sleeves. Gather lower end of sleeve to length of cuff (less underlap). Stitch and turn cuff and stitch on with underlap. Press hem under and stitch. Finally, make 2 loops on each cuff in buttonhole stitch and sew buttons in place on the underlap.

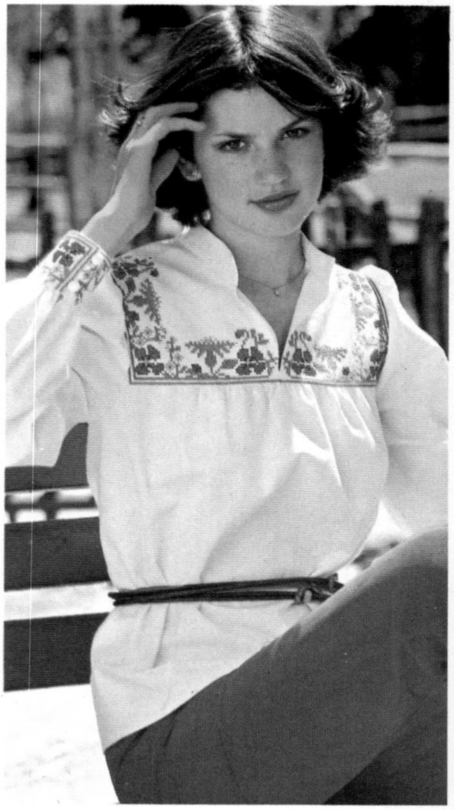

Inch equivalents:

	7.5 cm = 3″	15.5 cm = 6⅛″
	8 cm = 3⅛″	16.5 cm = 6⅝″
1.5 cm = ⅝″	8.5 cm = 3⅜″	17 cm = 6⅝″
2 cm = ¾″	9 cm = 3½″	17.5 cm = 7″
2.5 cm = 1″	9.5 cm = 3¾″	18.5 cm = 7⅜″
3 cm = 1⅛″	10 cm = 3⅞″	19 cm = 7½″
3.5 cm = 1⅜″	10.5 cm = 4⅛″	21 cm = 8¼″
4 cm = 1⅝″	11 cm = 4⅜″	26.5 cm = 10½″
4.5 cm = 1⅞″	12 cm = 4¾″	27 cm = 10¾″
5 cm = 2″	12.5 cm = 4⅞″	28 cm = 11⅛″
5.5 cm = 2¼″	13 cm = 5⅛″	38 cm = 15″
6 cm = 2⅜″	13.5 cm = 5⅜″	39 cm = 15⅜″
6.5 cm = 2⅝″	14 cm = 5½″	43.5 cm = 17⅛″
7 cm = 2¾″	15 cm = 5⅞″	46 cm = 18¼″

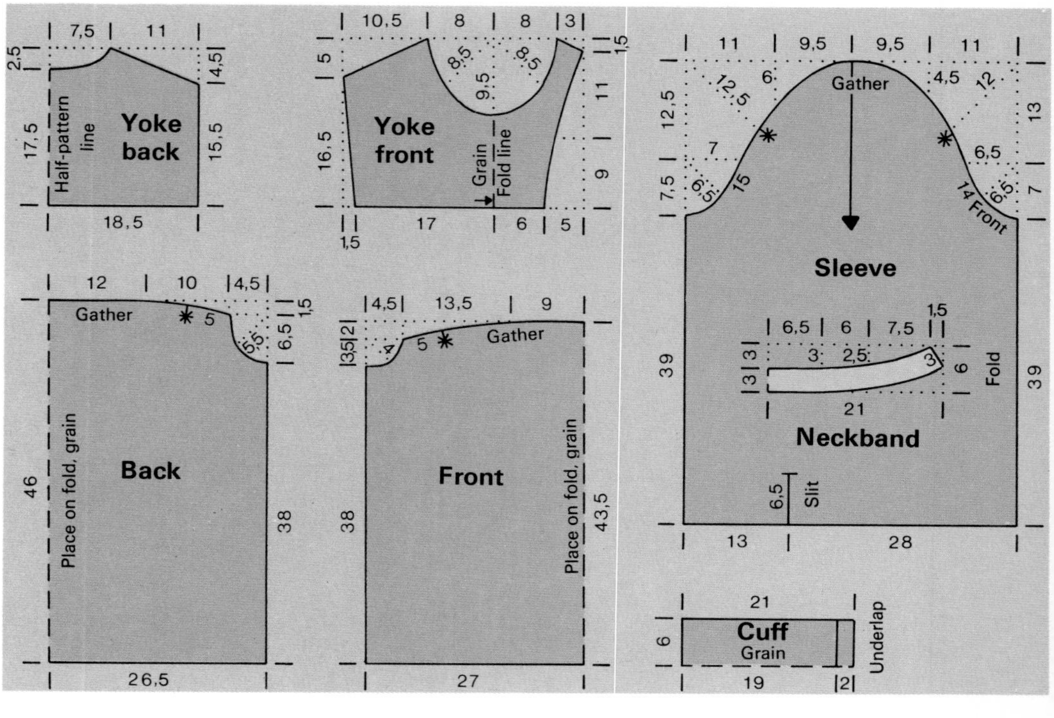

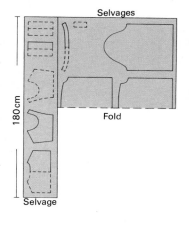

Floral display

Greet the first days of summer in a fresh white embroidered blouse with a flower border worked in cross-stitch.

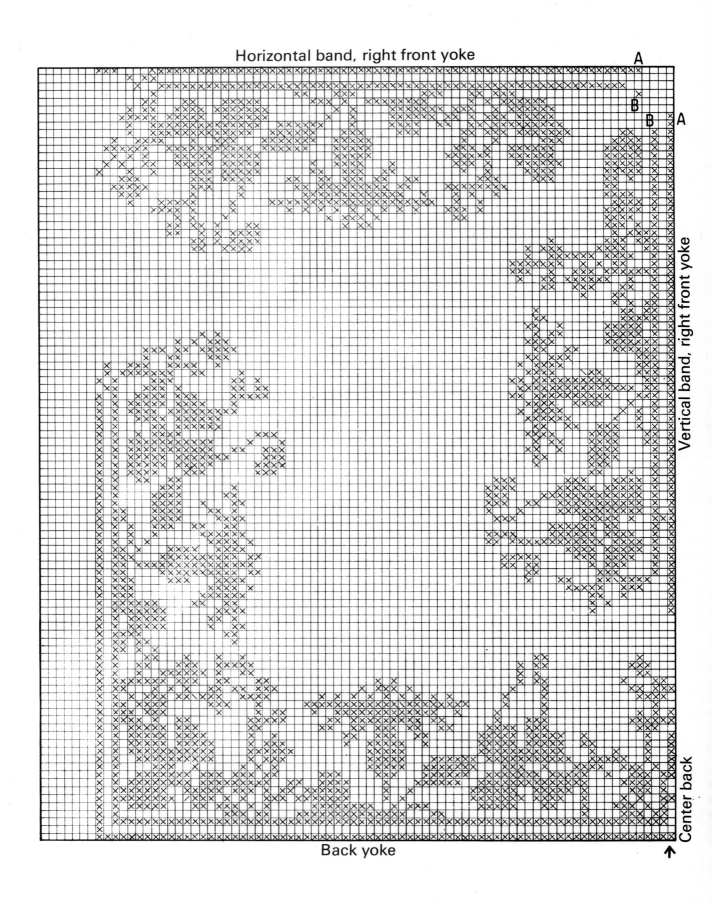

A

B

B A

Vertical band, right front yoke

Center back

Back yoke

To embroider in satin stitch

The delicate beauty of a rose

The full-blown rose motif looks beautiful on the pale cream background of this pure silk blouse. Stranded cotton is used to complement the delicate fabric. The motif can also be worked in subtle shades of rose and green to adorn accessories such as a handsome fringed shawl.

The stitch used to work the motif is a close satin stitch.

BLOUSE

Materials Required: 4 skeins stranded embroidery cotton to match blouse.

Basic Stitch: Satin stitch worked with 2 strands of stranded cotton.

Marking the design

Trace the rose motif onto transparent paper and transfer onto the fabric with dressmaker's carbon paper. To do this, place the dressmaker's carbon paper face down on the right side of the fabric with the traced motif on top. Hold both firmly in position and go over the outlines with a pencil. The transfer lines will be covered with embroidery.

Embroidering the motif

Fill in the outlines of each petal and leaf with closely worked satin stitch.

Satin stitch

Satin stitch is a decorative stitch which gives an almost three-dimensional effect of light and shade. It can be worked on many different kinds of fabric, and is used as a filling stitch. The stitches are worked straight or diagonally across the design, but wide areas should be divided into a series of short stitches to prevent very long stitches from forming.

Satin stitch can be worked from left to right or vice versa. It always follows the outline of the design and the needle is inserted at the top of the shape and emerges at the bottom.

When filling in wide shapes, however, the stitches should not be taken all the way across the outline as they will be too long to lie flat. Instead, the outer stitches are worked first, following the outline on one side, and staggering the lengths of the stitches toward the center. Fill in the center by taking the needle through the stitches already worked so that a hard edge is not formed. Again make the stitches different lengths. Finally, fill in the remaining side, following the outline of the design. This method of working the stitches into one another can also be used for shading where several colors are combined, but this requires practice so shading is not given on this motif.

1 Smaller, narrower motifs such as stems and stalks are filled in with vertical satin stitch.

2 Broader, oval-shaped motifs such as rosebuds are worked in diagonal satin stitch.

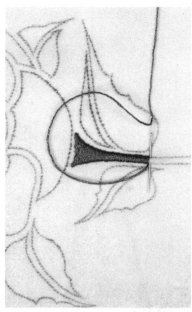

3 Large shapes such as petals and leaves are filled in with rows of interlocking satin stitch.

4 The reverse side of the work should look neat. Run threads under the stitches, clip ends.

Traditional floral motifs

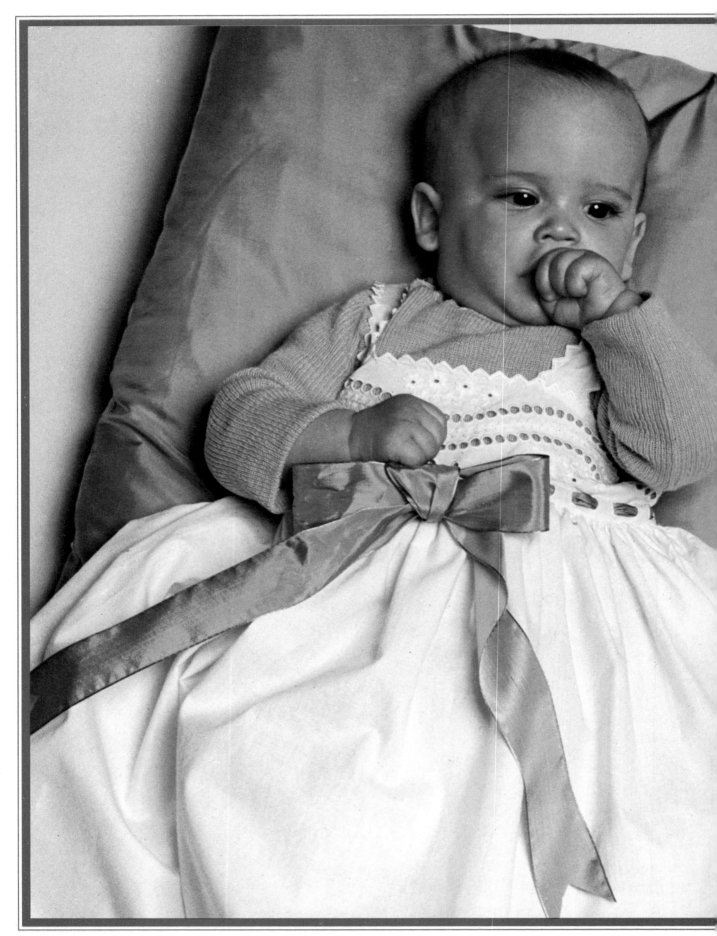

In cutwork or broderie anglaise

Dainty christening dress

This christening dress, with exquisite eyelet embroidery, is buttoned at the back of the yoke and trimmed with a ribbon. It is made in batiste which can be crisply starched.

Size: The christening dress will fit ages 1–9 months.

Materials Required:
White cotton batiste: 1.6 m (1¾ yds), 90 cm (36") wide. Ribbon: 2 m (2¼ yds), 4 cm (1½") wide. 4 buttons. White stranded cotton.

Cutting out

The cutting diagram for the yoke and straps is given on the following page. Cut out the yoke to the measurements given, adding a 1 cm (⅜") seam allowance at the lower edge. Cut out the strap twice, with a 1 cm (⅜") seam allowance at the ends.

For the skirt, cut two lengths of fabric 70 cm (27½") long by 90 cm (36") wide (ie, the fabric width). Cut the back skirt piece in half, cutting halfway between the two selvages.

Preparing for embroidery

Stitch the skirt side seams together close to the selvages, right sides facing. Then turn under the 2 raw edges at the center back opening twice, about 1.5 cm (⅝") each time. Stitch.

Working the embroidery

Trace the borders and eyelet holes from the pattern and transfer onto the lower edge of the skirt, the yoke, and the straps with dressmaker's carbon paper. Embroider with stranded cotton, using 2 strands for the outlining, padding, and detached chain stitches, and 4 strands for the scalloped edges and the chain stitch lines.

First work the long, curved lines and the flower stems in chain stitch, then work the flowers and leaves in detached chain or lazy daisy stitch.

The scalloped edges are first outlined with small running stitches, then filled in with staggered running stitches for padding. Finally, cover the outlines with buttonhole stitch.

Work the eyelet embroidery next. The outlines are again worked first with small running stitches and then covered with overcasting stitches. Taking care not to snip into the embroidery, trim eyelet holes, then cut off the excess fabric close to the scalloped line with very sharp scissors.

Making the dress

The seam allowance of the yoke back opening is included in the pattern. Turn under the seam allowance twice, making the second fold along the center back on one side and along the fold line indicated on the other side. Stitch.

Gather the skirt to fit the yoke and stitch in place. Trim the seam allowances to 0.5 cm (³⁄₁₆") and finish them together. Turn the seam allowances on the straps to the right side and stitch the straps to the yoke. Make 4 loops at the back of the yoke with stranded cotton for the buttons. Sew on the buttons. Cut the ribbon in half, sew to each half of the inside back opening and draw through the eyelet holes. Tie in a bow.

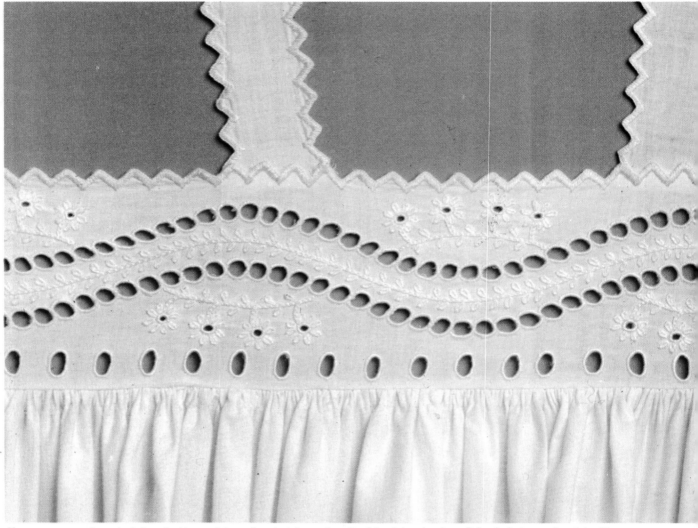

Above you can see the eyelet hole embroidery and the scalloped edging on the yoke of the christening dress. Below is the lower edge of the skirt.

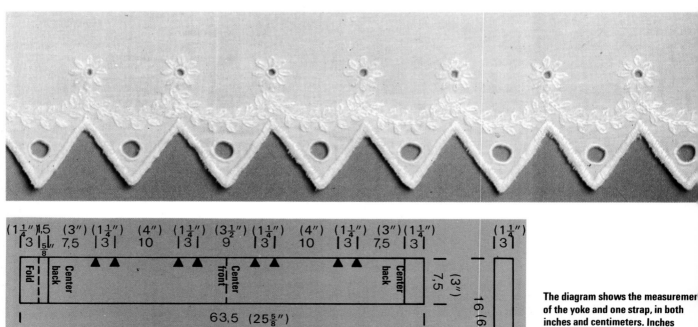

The diagram shows the measurement of the yoke and one strap, in both inches and centimeters. Inches are given in brackets. The arrows on the yoke indicate where the two straps should be positioned.

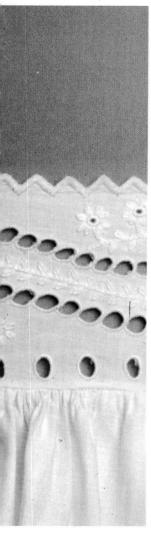

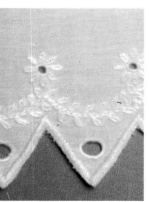

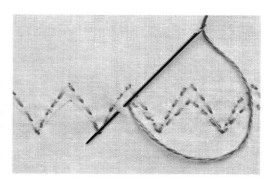

Scalloped edge in buttonhole stitch

1 Outline the scalloped edge with small running stitches, following the transferred lines. Work one zigzag line, and then the other.

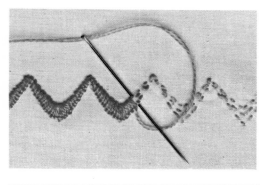

2 Fill in the lines with small running stitches for padding. Work over these with buttonhole stitch before cutting away the excess fabric.

Eyelet holes

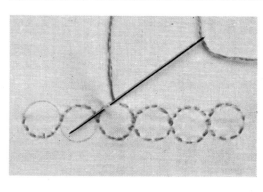

1 For the chains of eyelet holes, work running stitch along the outlines in two wavy lines, first from left to right, then from right to left.

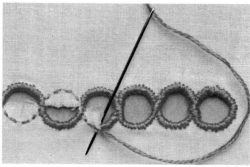

2 Cut a cross into each hole and turn under the fabric as you embroider. Work over the edge in wavy lines with close overcasting stitches. Trim off excess fabric at back.

Broderie anglaise borders

These charming openwork patterns are worked on the bodice, straps, and skirt edge of a dainty christening robe.

Our alphabet is delicate and ornate in white stranded embroidery cotton. Each letter is beautifully embroidered in stem stitch and padded satin stitch to make it stand out.

Alphabet in stem stitch and satin stitch

Take a letter...

E F G H

M N O P

U V W X

Embroidered script initials look smart and elegant on blouses, shirts, dresses, scarves, handkerchiefs, and bed linen, and never go out of fashion!

Interlocking monograms in relief are most effective worked in white on white. Pillow cases, the turn-back on sheets, or handkerchiefs will all have a more elegant look.

1

2

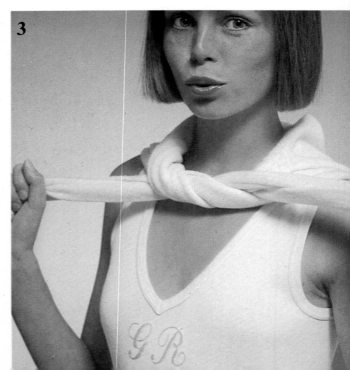

3

1 Something special: an initial on the beret and a decorative motif on the matching scarf.

2 Embroider your initials on the corners of a blouse collar.

3 A plain T-shirt or sports shirt can be boring. Give it an individual touch with embroidered initials.

4 A man's evening scarf becomes more distinctive with an embroidered monogram.

Embroidering initials

At one time, embroidered monograms adorned a young girl's trousseau. Today, they are a dainty and individual ornamentation on clothes and accessories. The wide areas of the letters are padded with filler stitches and appear to stand out in relief from the background. For this reason, white on white is very effective.

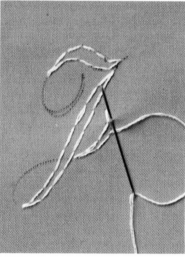

1 Preliminary stitch: Trace the outlines of the wide areas to be worked in satin stitch with closely-worked running stitches.

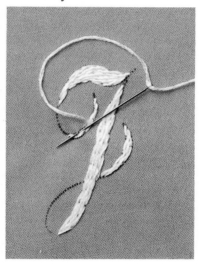

2 Padding stitches: Fill in the outlined areas with closely-worked running stitches to form a base for the satin stitch.

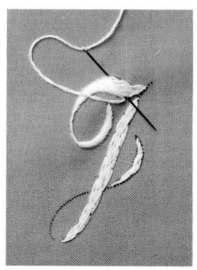

3 Satin stitch: Embroider over the padded areas with a slanting satin stitch, using two strands of stranded cotton.

4 Stem stitch: The fine lines of the letters are worked in stem stitch. The finished letter appears to stand out in relief.

Trace a letter

Embroidered monograms will look smart and elegant on everything from blouses, shirts, scarves, and berets to bed linen and handkerchiefs. Worked in white in stem stitch and padded satin stitch for a raised effect, they add a distinctive touch to your clothes and accessories.

Decorative embroidery can be
As simple as ABC

A B C D
I J K L S
P Q R S
W X Y

Here's an easy chain-stitch alphabet —
just right for initials and
monograms. Trace these embroidered
letters for actual-size patterns.

EFGH

MNO

STUV

Z

The Personal Touc

The charm of hand-embroidered initials will give clothes and accessories an individual look.

Delightful on children's clothes

Bright decoration on denim casuals

An embroidered tie for a special gift

A T-shirt with a touch of chic

A sporty letter for your favorite cap

Eye-catching jean embroidery

Personalized table linen for special occasions

New life for an old handbag

Chain stitch

Chain stitch is one of the oldest embroidery stitches – and one of the most versatile. It can be worked in single rows for outlining, in blocks of rows as a filling stitch, or as a detached stitch cluster for a pretty daisy motif.

Chain stitch is often used for working monograms and initials because its flexibility is ideal for embroidering along the curved lines of the letters. There are several chain stitch variations and the detached chain stitch or the lazy daisy stitch is shown here.

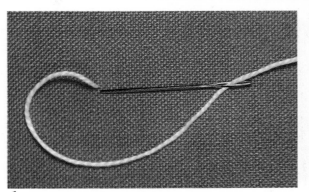

1 Work from right to left. Bring needle up through fabric and hold thread in a loop with your thumb. Reinsert needle at the point where it emerged.

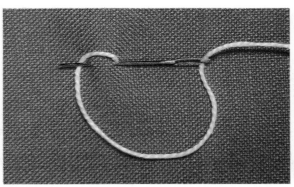

2 Bring needle point out a short distance away. Thread lies under needle point. When the needle and thread are pulled through, the chain is made.

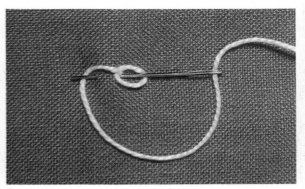

3 To make another chain stitch, reinsert needle at point where it emerged, bringing it out again the same distance away as for previous stitch.

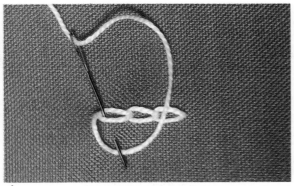

4 To change direction, bring the needle point out in the new direction and continue working chain stitches in the same way as for a horizontal line.

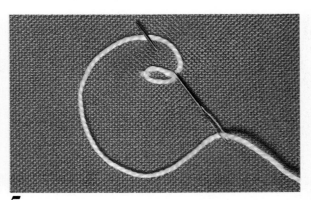

5 To make detached chain or lazy daisy stitch, make a chain and secure it with a tiny stitch. For round flower, work a circle of detached chains with a common base.

Motifs from A to Z

Alphabet letters are ideal for monograms, samplers and other decorative uses.

Working the embroidery

The alphabets illustrated are worked in cross-stitch on even-weave fabric. Each cross is worked over 2 threads each way, using 3 strands of stranded embroidery cotton. The top stitch of all the crosses should slant in the same direction. Count stitches for each design from the photograph.

The letters can also be embroidered onto fabric without a pronounced even weave by working the cross stitches over soft, fine canvas which is then withdrawn, thread by thread. The top alphabet is worked in a single color with a clover-shaped design left free to show the fabric beneath. The lower alphabet is given a shaded effect by filling in the letters with a paler color.

You can use the letters and the small interspersed motifs in a great variety of ways. For example, add a monogram to blouses, jeans, boleros, pullovers, and scarves. Design your own sampler or embroider a personal greetings card. By varying the thickness and color of thread and the weight of fabric, you can change the size and appearance of the letters to suit your purpose.

Shading with satin stitch

Picturesque posies

All these colorful flowers
are given on a trace pattern and
can easily be transferred with
dressmaker's carbon paper. The
subtle, shaded effect is achieved by
embroidering them with satin
stitches of unequal length in
cleverly chosen variations of color.
The finished flowers look as
delicate as a painting.

The important feature of needle "painting" is the delicate shading which produces the effect of a real painting. The length of the stitches is graduated, so that the shades of color blend in with one another. Use your own flair for color to choose the subtlest of tones.

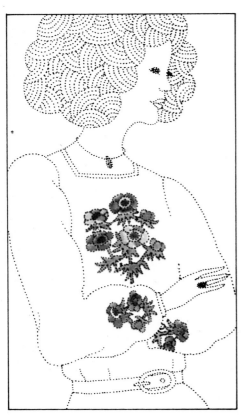

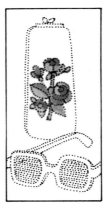

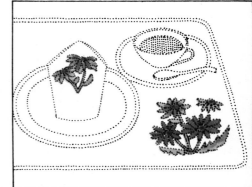

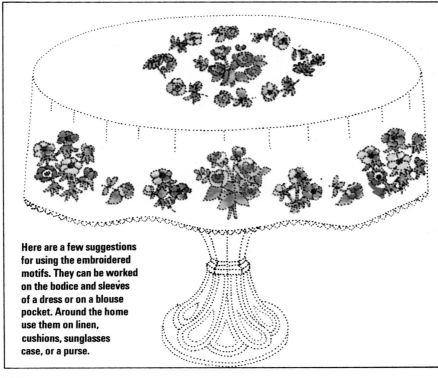

Here are a few suggestions for using the embroidered motifs. They can be worked on the bodice and sleeves of a dress or on a blouse pocket. Around the home use them on linen, cushions, sunglasses case, or a purse.

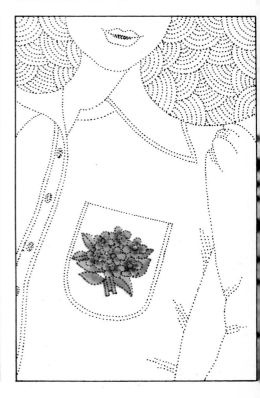

Materials Required:
Stranded cotton. Each motif needs only small amounts, so use remnants.

Anemones
Pale pink
Medium pink
Dark pink
Scarlet
Wine red
Lemon yellow
Pale grey
Dark grey
Pale blue
Medium blue
Sky blue
Dark purple
Brown
Pale green
Dark green

Marguerites
Scarlet
Dark pink
Lemon yellow
Sun yellow
Dark gold
Light reddish-brown
Dark brown
Pale green
Medium green
Dark green

Roses
Pale rose
Dark rose
Medium pink
Crimson
Deep wine red
Pale green
Medium green
Dark green
Rose madder
Carmine

Violets
Dark purple
Sun yellow
Pale green
Medium green
Dark green
Pale turquoise
Dark turquoise

Pansies
Pale Grey
Pale blue
Medium blue
Dark purple
Gold
Pale green
Medium green
Dark green
Pale turquoise
Dark turquoise
Blue-green

Basic Stitch: Satin stitch with 3 strands of cotton.

Shading with satin stitch

1 Begin at the outer edge of the motif and work a section in varying stitch lengths.

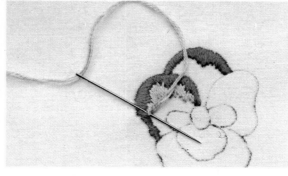

2 Work the next color so that it interlocks with the embroidered section.

3 Fill in larger areas of a single color with long and short satin stitch.

4 Here you can see two petals and the center of the pansy completed.

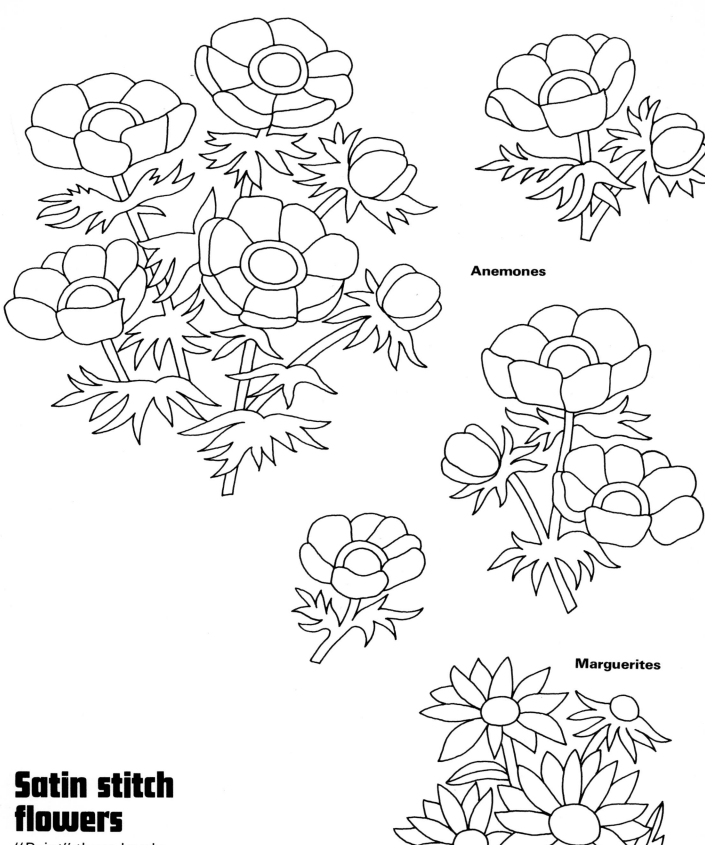

Anemones

Marguerites

Satin stitch flowers

''Paint'' these lovely
flowers with your
needle. Embroider them
in interlocking areas
of satin stitch in
light and dark shades.

Violets

Roses

Pansies

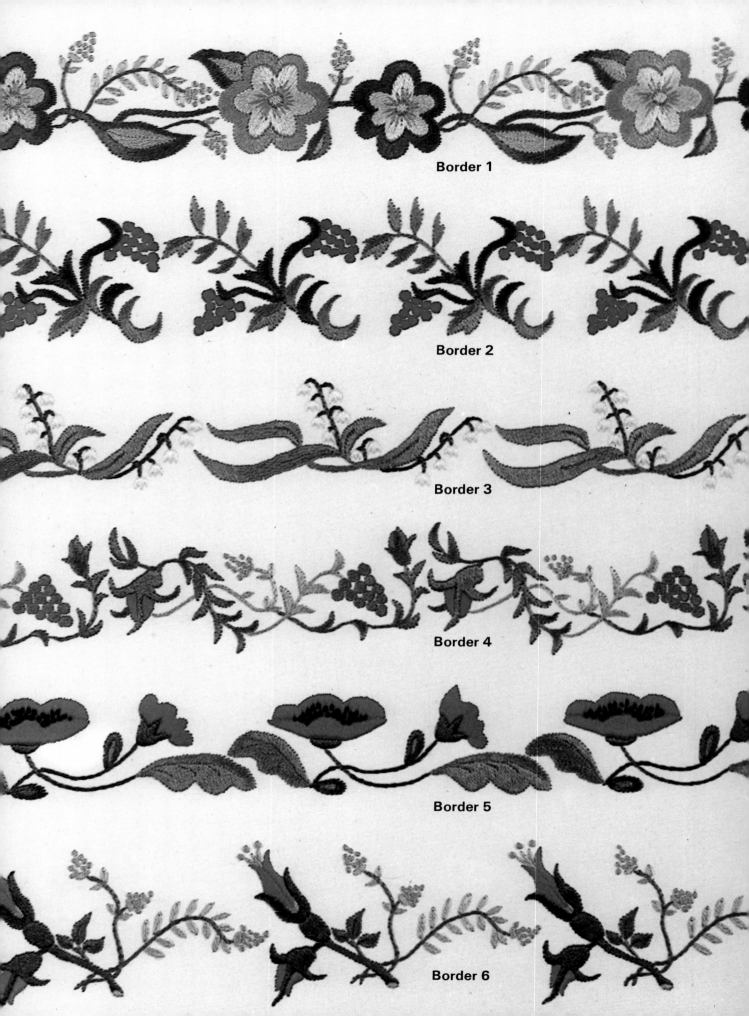

Border 1

Border 2

Border 3

Border 4

Border 5

Border 6

Flower power

Delicate floral borders are a delightful way to decorate clothes and accessories. See them spring to life with each stitch as you embroider.

Posy

Floral borders

Here are some ideas for embroidered borders which can be used in lots of different ways. Add one to a smock or headscarf, or decorate a set of napkins and matching tablecloth.

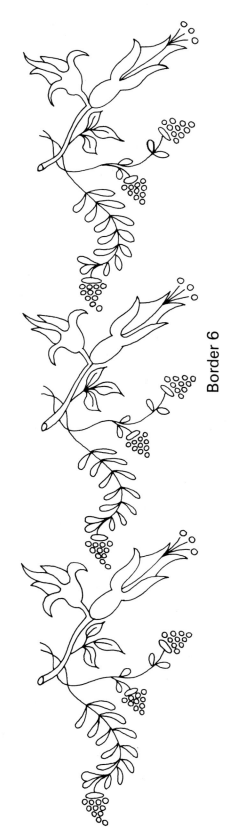

Border 6

Border 2

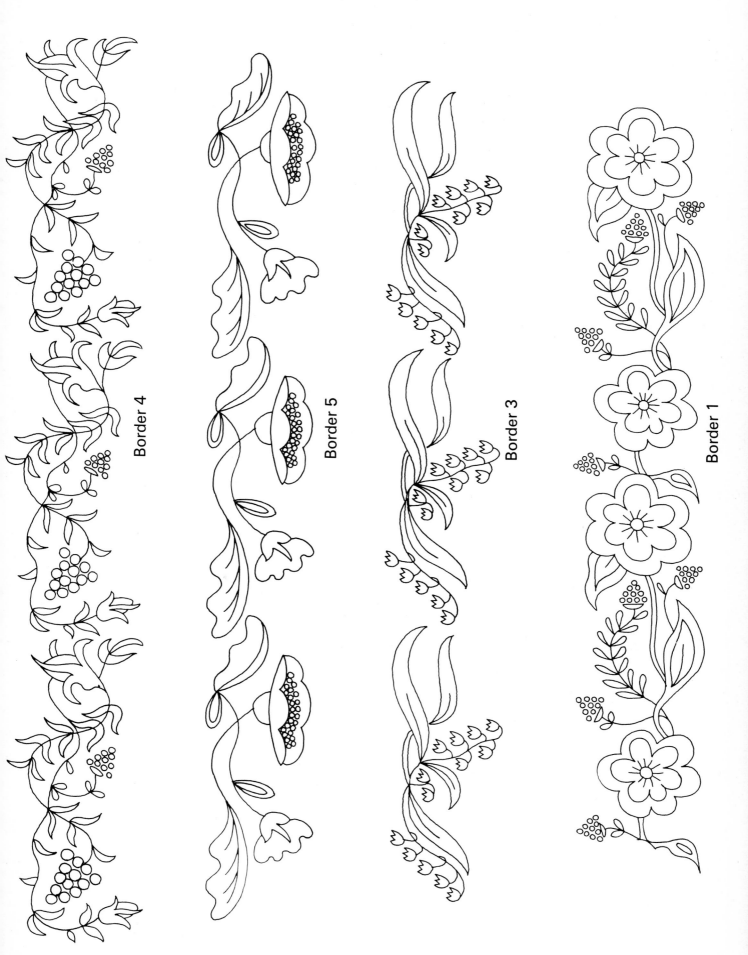

Border 4

Border 5

Border 3

Border 1

1

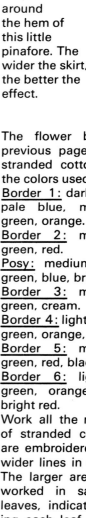

2

3

4

A bright red berry border is embroidered around the hem of this little pinafore. The wider the skirt, the better the effect.

1 Embroider the red poppies around the edges of a head scarf, then tie it at the back of the head to make a face-flattering accessory.

2 A floral climber decorates one cushion and a posy the other to bring shades of summer into your home all year round.

3 A garland of blue flowers trims the wide, fluttering sleeves of a summer blouse in a fine fabric.

4 For a unique accessory, embroider a clutch bag with delicate lilies-of-the-valley. They look especially pretty on a pale green background.

The flower borders on the two previous pages were worked with stranded cotton. Here is a list of the colors used for each border.
Border 1: dark blue, medium blue, pale blue, medium green, light green, orange.
Border 2: medium green, dark green, red.
Posy: medium green, dark moss green, blue, bright red, orange.
Border 3: medium green, dark green, cream.
Border 4: light moss green, medium green, orange, blue, bright red.
Border 5: medium green, dark green, red, black.
Border 6: light green, medium green, orange, dark moss green, bright red.
Work all the motifs with 2 strands of stranded cotton. The thin lines are embroidered in stem stitch, the wider lines in diagonal satin stitch. The larger areas and dots are also worked in satin stitch. For the leaves, indicate the veins by working each leaf section separately in satin stitch so that an indentation appears where the sections meet. Alternatively, work the veins in stem stitch, the leaves in diagonal satin stitch. In Border 1, work the rays at the flower centers in straight stitch in a deeper color. The small dots are French knots.

INDEX